A Voice from the Holocaust

Eve Nussbaum Soumerai and
Carol D. Schulz

Voices of Twentieth-Century Conflict

Greenwood Press
Westport, Connecticut • London

Library of Congress Cataloging-in-Publication Data

Soumerai, Eve Nussbaum.
  A voice from the Holocaust / by Eve Nussbaum Soumerai and Carol D. Schulz.
       p.   cm.—(Voices of twentieth-century conflict)
     Includes bibliographical references and index.
     ISBN 0–313–32358–5 (alk. paper)
     1. Holocaust, Jewish (1939–1945)—Personal narratives—Juvenile
  literature.   2. Holocaust, Jewish (1939–1945)—Study and teaching
  (Secondary).   3. Germany—History—1933–1945—Juvenile
  literature.   I. Schulz, Carol D., 1948–   II. Title.   III. Series.
  D804.3.S64   2003
  940.53'18—dc21   2003045528

British Library Cataloguing-in-Publication Data is available.

Library of Congress Catalog Card Number: 2003045528
ISBN: 0–313–32358–5

First published in 2003.

Greenwood Press, 88 Post Road West, Westport, CT 06881
An imprint of Greenwood Publishing Group, Inc.
www.greenwood.com

Printed in the United States of America

The paper used in this book complies with the
Permanent Paper Standard issued by the National
Information Standards Organization (Z39.48–1984).

10 9 8 7 6 5 4 3 2 1

Still Immersed in My Parents' Gifts

Mama: . . . Ich musste doch lachen dass Du jetzt Papa's Rolle uebernomer hast und Geschichten erzaelst mit so viel Erfolgt . . .

. . . I have to laugh that you have taken over Papa's role and tell stories with so much success . . .

Papa: (same letter) Ich wollte, ich koennte Dir bald wieder eine schoene lange Geschichte erzaehlen. Die Zeit wird kommen, I muss nur warten . . .

I wish I could tell you a long beautiful story again. The time will come. I just have to wait. . . . Letter dated December 28, 1940 . . .

I have never stopped telling stories and laughing with children.

—*Eve Nussbaum Soumerai*

Contents

Contents

Contents

To the Teacher

As a middle and high school history teacher, I have spent years trying to find books that excite students. As good as some textbooks can be, even the best among them provide more facts and statistics than engaging stories. Historical fiction sometimes fills the gap, but it is, after all, fiction. History needs to be vivid and alive if we are to capture the attention of students. That is the intention of the Voices of Twentieth-Century Conflict series.

The series focuses on significant periods and events of the twentieth century, e.g. the Holocaust and the Vietnam War. Each volume is a primary source that looks at a historical period through the eyes of one individual. Most of the stories in the series occurred when the authors were children and young adults. Through personal vignettes and reflections, they reveal the ways in which global events challenged their beliefs and changed their lives forever.

To create a context for each story, an introduction, a timeline, a glossary, and brief historical essays are included. And, of course, each volume includes photographs, maps, or other graphics that will engage young adult readers.

At the end of each book are questions and projects that encourage students to make connections between their own lives and the life of the author and that invite them to reflect on the universal themes raised in the text.

Most important, the stories in this series demonstrate clearly that we live in a global community, and that the choices each one of us makes can have profound consequences, not just for ourselves, but for everyone—even those we have yet to meet.

In an age when students require both critical thinking skills and historical perspective to make wise choices, the authors and I believe that this engaging and thought-provoking series will meet this crucial need.

Carol D. Schulz

Foreword

I first met Eve Soumerai in the summer of 1980, while working on my master's thesis at Wesleyan University. I was writing about the Holocaust, trying to make some kind of sense out of this horrifying piece of history. Eve was the first "survivor" I spoke with. Although she had not spent time in the concentration camps and, in fact, did not even think of herself as a survivor of the Holocaust, I knew she had much to tell me. I was nervous, worried that I would be making her talk about events she didn't want to think about. But she welcomed me into her home, fed me (of course), and shared her memories with me of the wonderful life she had led before the Nazis came along, and of the disintegration of that life when Hitler came to power.

That was the start of more than twenty years of friendship, learning, teaching, and collaborating. We have worked together helping students and their teachers celebrate the lives of their heroes—writers, statesmen, and musicians, from Anne Frank to Paul Robeson—in the creation of dramatic tributes. We have taught workshops on the need to embrace differences and respect the rights of all people. And we have co-authored books about human rights and the Holocaust. Our friendship has been a wonderful adventure.

This book is Eve's story. It contains brief passages on historical background (that's my contribution) that should enable your students to understand the context of the events described, without their having to turn to outside resources. Most of all, it is the story of one girl's experiences in Europe during the most painful years of the twentieth century. It is not a morbid tale, nor is it depressing, although it is very sad. Eve speaks to young adults because she writes about her life as a teenager, facing ordinary "teenager" problems during extraordinary times: wanting to fit in, needing to feel loved, having to forge an identity.

We hope your students will read this volume, reflect on what they have discovered, and in some way find meaning here. I am not really certain that anyone learns lessons from history, but if this is possible, I hope that, should they ever find themselves alone in the world, with no family, friends, or anyone to offer comfort and encouragement, they will have learned to reach out—not to ask for help from others, but to offer it to those in need. That is what Eve did, and that is how she found a new world of friends and family with whom to share her life.

The historian Yehuda Bauer writes that because of the Holocaust, three new commandments were created: "Thou shalt not be a victim. Thou shalt not be a perpetrator. Above all, thou shalt not be a bystander." These, too, are lessons to be learned.

Carol D. Schulz

Preface

. . . And the thoughts of youth are long, long thoughts.
—*Longfellow*

I hold on to the "long, long thoughts" of my youth every day. That way, my parents and brother will never disappear. Let me introduce you to Papa, my father, Berthold; Mama, my mother, Frieda; Norbert, my brother, also called Bibi. He is a year and a bit younger than me. I am the only daughter, Eva, and I am about to leave them forever. Only, I don't know it's forever. I think it's only for a year. Would I have left them if I had known? I don't think so. Would I have left them had I known they would be tortured and suffer slow, horrible deaths? I don't know. I really don't know.

I do know that I want you to meet them as I knew them those first thirteen years of my life, and then you will understand why I hold on to them for dear life. We'll go backward and forward. We'll be untidy. Think about it—Isn't that how your innermost feelings and your heart work, moving all over the place without rhyme or reason?

We will start with my departure from home at age thirteen, the defining moment of my life, and then go backward to my happiest years; then we will move forward through the unhappy ones, so very unhappy that there came a day I no longer wanted to get up from bed. You will learn that the years of my childhood are gifts from my parents. I will refer to my parents as Papa and Mama—that's what I called them, until I became responsible, at age fifteen. Then, I will refer to them as "my father" and "my mother" to indicate my feelings of pride and gratitude.

You might wonder about all those quotes I've added. I include them because most of them were written by good, caring people, and discovering them helped me become less lonely. The few words in this book written by evil people helped me understand the nature of evil and to look for ways to do *tikkun olam*—Hebrew for "healing the world." For me, this meant spending as much time with children as I could. Making them happy made me happy, too.

Eve Nussbaum Soumerai

Acknowledgments

There is hope.

This hope lies in individuals such as Rochelle Holder and Alain Lopez to whom I dedicate this memoir.

Their untiring efforts have helped me, the lonely refugee child, give expression to the gifts my family gave me for the benefit of many, including my parents' grandchildren, their children and those to come.

Rochelle and Alain are kindred spirits. They see the need for belonging and family in today's world. We become Big Brothers and Sisters to children of all ages, celebrating and paying tribute to the lives of inspirational individuals such as Thurgood Marshall and Anne Frank, who become part of our family. We compose read-through plays about them, sing their songs, and illustrate their lives.

Rochelle, choir director in Hartford, Connecticut schools for thirty-eight years, has for the past twelve years added music to our tribute celebrations. She always starts with the old African echo song "We're On Our Way" and ends each celebration with her rendition of "God Bless the Child."

Alain, senior at Trinity College, demonstrated his intuitive love for *los ninos* during his freshman year in high school in the South Bronx. He "fell in love" working with the five- and six-year-olds at the Mott Haven community center. At Trinity College, he researched and wrote a tribute to his hero Jose Marti and led a group of interested students to the Boys and Girls Club to offer children this type of "fun" education.

I was happy in Nazi Germany. The evil of the regime affected us daily, but my family's love and attention was like heavy armor protecting me. At thirteen, I left them forever in a crowded railroad station knowing goodness and evil exist side by side, but that goodness is stronger.

And then something new entered my life, the experience of being a refugee child. All-consuming loneliness became my daily companion, sapped my energy, and, worse, made me long for oblivion. One day my guardians bundled me up and sent me to a residential nursery school for evacuated children. Miraculously, it was there that I discovered my love for children and met my first kindred spirit, Maureen, almost five years old. She made me aware that these spirits exist at any age and in the oddest places, making the seemingly impossible possible. Together, we are determined to spread the case for goodness and laughter so that *all may know they are not alone.*

Introduction

On January 30, 1933, Adolf Hitler became the Chancellor of Germany when his political party, the National Socialist German Workers' Party, or Nazis, helped him win a plurality in the election for parliament. From that day until their surrender at the conclusion of World War II, the German government waged a war against the Jews of Europe, first depriving them of their rights as citizens, then of their right to freedom, and finally of their right to life.

On September 1, 1939, the German army invaded Poland. Two days later Great Britain declared war on Germany. By June 1940 nearly all of Western and Central Europe was under Nazi rule. That summer, massive bombing raids on England took place. Hitler planned to weaken and then invade the island nation. In his now famous speech to the House of Commons, Prime Minister Winston Churchill told his countrymen, "I have nothing to offer but blood, toil, tears and sweat." From July to October, the Royal Air force successfully beat back the Germans, losing 915 planes to the Luftwaffe's 1722.

By the summer of 1941, most of Eastern Europe and Greece were conquered. Only Russia remained standing.

On May 7, 1945, the Allied forces, under the command of American General Dwight D. Eisenhower, defeated the German army. Twelve years, four months, and eight days after he had taken power, Hitler's reign of terror was over.

Nearly 6,000,000 Jewish people, two-thirds of those who lived in Europe at the time, perished under Nazi rule. Of all the countries in the world, Great Britain was the only one willing to provide a haven for Jewish children. In a program called the Kindertransport, 10,000 children—kinder—were saved before the war began and the gates were closed. The 1.5 million kinder left behind were murdered.

On June 30, 1939, thirteen-year-old Eva Nussbaum said goodbye to her family and began her journey to England as a refugee from Nazi Germany.

Carol D. Schulz

Timeline

1933

January 30   Adolf Hitler becomes chancellor of Germany.

February 27   The Reichstag is set on fire and Hitler blames the Communists.

March 20   Dachau, the first concentration camp, is created.

March 27   The Enabling Act is passed, giving Hitler absolute power.

April   Official persecution of the Jews begins.

1934

August 2   President Paul von Hindenburg dies. The office of President is abolished. Hitler becomes Reich Chancellor and the Fuehrer (Leader) of Germany.

1935

September 15   Nuremberg Race Laws passed. Jews are no longer considered citizens of Germany.

1938

July 6–15   Representatives of thirty-two countries meet at Evian, France to decide what to do about Jews who need to leave Germany. Only the Dominican Republic agrees to provide sanctuary for additional Jews.

October 28   Thousands of Polish Jews living in Germany are expelled; they are forced to live in refugee camps between Poland and Germany.

November 9–10   On "Crystal Night," the German government supports a nationwide pogrom that destroys thousands of synagogues, Jewish stores, and businesses; 20,000 Jewish men are sent to concentration camps.

December 1   The first train of the Kindertransport leaves Germany.

1939

September 1   Germany invades Poland; World War II begins.

September 3   Great Britain declares war against Germany.

1941

October   The first groups of German and Austrian Jews are deported. By 1942, Eve's parents and her brother, along with the rest of her family still in Germany, have been deported to Poland.

December 11   Germany declares war on the United States and our nation joins the Allies in their fight against Nazi Germany and the Axis powers.

1942

January 20   At the Wannsee Conference, Nazi officials meet
                to plan the details of the "final solution to the
                Jewish question."

1944

June 6   The Allies invade Normandy.

1945

April 30   Hitler commits suicide.

May 7   Germany surrenders to the Allies.

Departure

Hope is the thing with feathers,
That perches in the soul
And sings the tune without the words—
And never stops—at all.

—Emily Dickinson

Fare thee well!
and if forever . . .
fare thee well.

—Lord Byron

June 30, 1939

It was well past ten at night when we snuck off to the Tiergarten (the park near us) for one last time. The sky was dark, the color of ink. Stars hovered so close above us that we could almost touch them. Papa pointed to his favorite constellation, the Big Dipper. "Looks like a saucepan without a lid," was Bibi's view. *Why did he have to stay and I leave? He had often wanted to be included with my friends. I would call him a baby and leave him out. Why?* Mama was so very sad. I gave her the poem I wrote that I knew she would like.

Dance, dance Mama, dance
The Chestnut tree is in bloom
Waiting to embrace you. Evchen for Mama

Mama actually swung her hips and danced. Papa smiled. We were having a party. "Take three deep breaths and make a wish," ordered Papa. "Mine is that by spring, in less than a year, we'll be looking at the same stars over Central Park." Bibi was next: "Maybe then you'll let me belong to a boxing club." We knew Mama's secret before she told us, "That we see each other for sure, for sure." In a place where there is less hate is what I wished for, but I did not tell.

Later, Mama came in and out of my room all evening, unable to sit or speak. On one of those trips she opened my suitcase and added two carefully wrapped gifts for "Uncle" and "Auntie," my temporary guardians in England. I told her not to worry and reminded her that a year is nothing.

Papa sat on my bed for the last time ever. I looked at his kind and laughing eyes and at the suitcase with that brand new hat on top waiting by the door, and suddenly I decided that leaving was not for me. I did not want to go. "That's all right," Papa said. "If you feel like this in the morning, you can stay."

The next day the morning sun tickled my nose and woke me. It was a glorious spring morning. I was only thirteen years old, but I felt very grown up; that is, until we reached the crowded waiting room at the Anhalter Station. Seeing the crying parents and their children clutching dolls and teddy bears, all squashed together like sardines, made me very uneasy. What was happening to us? A young couple standing next to Bibi tried in vain to pacify their noisy, young son who kept trying to run off. "He'll never know us," said the sobbing mother while the father finally managed to push a lollipop into the little boy's mouth. The ensuing lull gave Bibi the opportunity to tell me once again to send him a pair of boxing gloves, and if I could find a Mickey Mouse balloon he would hang it from the ceiling next to his bed. It would remind him of America. "That's where Mickey Mouse comes from," he said.

Mama reminded me again to say thank you for "everything" to Uncle and Auntie, and to take good care of my new clothes. Then she added something new: "Cut your toenails regularly, else they grow into the flesh." Papa, my best friend ever, added, "Remember to laugh and play even when you are lost and sad." It was all too much. I again decided to stay with them, come what may. Papa intercepted my thoughts.

"You know what?" he asked.

"What?"

"As soon as I get home, I promise I'll write you a long letter and include a more grown-up photo of Bibi." Papa's last words. My Papa, who had always been there for me at all hours of the day and night, and who had never, ever suggested in words, looks, or deeds that I needed any kind of improvement.

My name, Eva Nussbaum, was called over the loudspeaker. Bibi looked wilted.

"Maybe I can live near you," he said.

"I promise, I'll ask."

I hugged Mama. She managed a smile, while tears ran down her face.

"Look at the stars and moon, and pray," she whispered, as though talking to herself.

I left and did not look back. My eyes and nose were running. My new patent leather shoes sounded like the beats of a drum. I don't remember how I got into the train. I just remember the doors clapping shut behind me and the train whistling.

Part I

Back to the Beginning

My Name Is Evchen

Family is the last and greatest discovery.
It is our last miracle.

—*James McBride*

Goodness and truth, the supreme aims for which man
should live and work.

—*Tolstoy*

"You arrived in the golden glow of the morning sun, at 6:30 in the morning, Saturday, May 15, 1926," Mama reminded me on each of my birthdays. "I sang 'Weisst Du wie viel Sterne stehen an dem blauen Himmelszelt?' [Do you know how many stars there are in the blue heaven's tent?] while you were growing in my tummy." That's how she made sure I would love music and wonder about the stars in God's heaven. "Nobody knows how many stars there really are, and that's the truth," she proclaimed with conviction. "Some are so far away, you cannot see them, but they are there."

Not only was I born in the golden glow of the morning sun, but I also emerged on the Sabbath. (In the Jewish religion the Sabbath falls on Saturday and is a day for rest, family and joy.) This was a fortuitous omen because it is when the family gathers to light candles, sip wine, and break bread. According to tradition, Sabbath angels accompany the newborn child's entry into the family, and "Who knows," said Opa, Mama's father and the official keeper of our faith, "they may stay and protect you throughout your life." Besides, I was born under the sign of Taurus, the bull, and I would therefore be strong, stubborn, and fiercely loyal. I totally believed in the bull, and when Mama complained of my being too willful, I reminded her that I was Taurus's baby.

The name on my birth certificate is Eva. It was a popular name

Evchen, taken in the Tiergarten, 1927; this copy decorated
widow "Omachen's" (my father's mother) night stand.

in the 1920s, comparable to Ashley or Brittany now. Evchen was
my nickname, a term of endearment. My "Evchen" photograph
was taken in our beloved Tiergarten when I was barely a year old.
Of course I do not remember the occasion, but because everybody
vaguely connected with my family received a copy, I grew up
with this image.

A life-sized version of this photograph in a golden frame was displayed on Opa and Oma's grand piano next to my parents' wedding photo in a matching frame. Papa carried a smaller version in his wallet and Mama used a copy as a bookmark, which, I thought, "moved" much too slowly through Tolstoy's *War and Peace*.

I didn't like that book and remember asking Mama to hurry up and put "me" in a book with happy stories instead of stories of torture. I still remember two vivid illustrations. One was of a decorated Napoleon, short and potbellied, riding his white horse by some lake and commanding his army to direct cannon fire at the thick ice beneath the feet of handsome Russian cavalry soldiers on elegant horses. The other illustration showed the soldiers and the horses in various positions of agonizing deaths in those icy waters. "Tolstoy wanted a good world, that's the reason for these stories," said Mama. "And that's what all good people want, Evchen."

Earliest Memory

All beings and all things shall be as relatives.
—Sioux Indian

The other ducks were in the yard and looked at the
new little duckling: Oh fie, how ugly that one is, we
will not endure him ... And immediately one of the
ducks flew at him and bit him on the neck. ...
—Hans Christian Andersen

It must have been because of the white duck with the gray
stripes that I have such a clear memory of this particular occasion.
My brother had just been born and suddenly I had to share center

The entire family; I am almost two, my brother Norbert is six
months.

stage with him. But Quack-Quack, my duck, was all mine. She followed me wherever I went. All I had to do was pull.

Decked out in our Sunday best, we were taking our Sunday stroll in the Tiergarten, where we met a roving photographer who offered to take our photograph. But my very own Quack-Quack was missing and I began to fuss. Papa found her "hiding" behind the big oak tree and placed her in front of me, while he and Mama held my hands for reassurance.

At bedtime Papa read to me, once again, the story of the Ugly Duckling while I glanced at Quack Quack, who was "listening" in the corner. That's how I learned that ugly ducklings were really beautiful swans.

My Father

Music and rhythm find their way into the secret places of the soul.

—*Plato*

Wer reitet so spaet durch Nacht und Wind?
Es ist der Vater mit seinem Kind.
Er haelt den Knaben wohl in dem Arm,
Er haelt ihn sicher er haelt ihn warm . . .

Who is it, that rides so very late
   through the night and the wind?
It is the father and his child.
He holds the young boy tight in his arms.
He holds him safe and warm . . .

—*Goethe*

When I heard Eddie Fisher croon "Oh My Papa" from the cream-colored radio sitting on the kitchen counter in my home in Springfield, Massachusetts, I was instantly transported into the dancing arms of my Papa, who was saving Evchen, his little girl, from the fatal promises of Goethe's "Erlking," and promising eternal play with his beautiful daughter.

I felt the galloping horse ride faster and faster through the night and the wind, listening to all the promises. I, too, die at the end of the poem—but not really, because Papa kept reciting the lines over and over while we continued riding through the woods, making *Tot* (death) a temporary condition, a mere rhyming word. Plus, for Papa's little girl, *Tot* always led to that special hug and tickle, invariably resulting in peals of laughter—the real ending of the poem.

That's how I learned that words, combined with rhythm, love, and laughter, stay with you and become beacons of light during life's darkest days.

My Father's Parents

Life is meeting—when we relate to others.
—*Martin Buber*

I never met them in person, but my father told so many stories about his parents that they became a part of who I am.

The night before I left Germany, Papa gave me a photo of them taken in the Eilenriede, the big park in Hannover, where they lived and where he (Berthold), his four brothers (Karl, Adolf, Max, and Leo), and his sister (Friedel) were born.

Hannchen and Nathan Nussbaum were happy. You can tell from the following photo taken in 1919, shortly after World War I. Few men at that time took their wives to the park to have a beer, let alone to have their photo taken. To have had happy, loving grandparents (and parents) is more important than most people realize. Today, this photo graces my wall. I pass it every time I go up the stairs. I look at grandfather's pocket watch with the gold chain, which he received from the city of Hannover for apprenticing many youths during a time of severe unemployment, teaching them the technique of recycling scrap iron.

Grandmother's hat is decorated with a flower. She loved flowers and grew them with herbs and vegetables on the small plot of land behind their cottage, which also served as workplace. Herbs, carrots, cabbages, onions, and potatoes, along with bits of meat, stewed all day long in a pot on the back of the stove in the kitchen. Grandmother always had a cup of soup and a piece of yesterday's bread for family as well as strangers. Fresh bread was too expensive for all the mouths she had to feed. They were considered "poor" compared to Mama's parents, "but they were really rich," claimed my father. They were always surrounded by friends and hungry acquaintances.

Hannchen and Nathan Nussbaum wearing their Sunday best and enjoying themselves in the Eilenriede, Hannover, 1918.

Grandfather was very ethical. He refused to endanger the lives of his apprentices and insisted on detonating leftover grenades, plentiful after the war. The family was always worried. One sunlit, frosty Sunday morning, one of those grenades detonated, tearing off both his hands. Someone with a horse and carriage to take him to the hospital could not be located in time. He bled to death. He had almost saved enough money to buy two horses and a carriage, which would have saved his life.

Where We Come From

I greet you at the beginning of a great career, which
must have had a long foreground somewhere . . .
                              —*R. W. Emerson to Walt Whitman*

Eating is the best kind of praying.
                              —*Yiddish proverb*

Grandparents and parents make up the long "foreground" in
our lives, whether we have great or not-so-great careers. Let me
list the "characters" of my life story. My father, the storyteller,
and my mother, the poet, are the principals. He laughed a lot; she
sighed. He explained life's complexities in words easy to understand; she "felt the truth," and found refuge in poems, trees, stars,
the heavens, a few chosen recipes, and God.

I was sure the chestnut tree outside our living room window
had a connection to my mother, from its lacy candlelike blossoms
in the spring to its prickly burrs enclosing the nuts in the fall,
which we loved to collect and polish. Mama would gaze long and
lovingly at the tiny miracles, the stars, appearing between its
branches most evenings. Papa, on the other hand, fitted the stars
into constellations and told us their stories. My favorite was about
Orion, the hunter. How his blind eyes were healed by the sun's
rays and how you could always locate him in the sky by his shiny
belt.

Of course, *der liebe Gott* (dearest God, that's what we called
Him) was in charge of creation. Proof, in case we were doubters,
were the crocuses and snowdrops that emerged each spring
through the frozen earth, sometimes carrying loads of heavy snow
on their petals. In early March we would visit "our" crocus patch
in the Tiergarten to see for ourselves. I remember picking a bunch

and thinking how strong their tiny, fragile stems were; while I could not even make a dent pushing the earth with my pointer finger, even though I pushed down from the outside, these little stems had to push up from the inside.

Mama claimed food was almost as important as the stars and the trees. She had two recipes on which she relied. The first was Schmorbraten (beef pot roast), which she smothered with onions, carrots, and parsnips. "Lots of onions," she declared. These fruits of paradise, she claimed, not only give off heavenly odors, but bring forth the unique flavor of the ingredients. I loved to sneak a look at the bubbling mixture in the ancient, iron, black-sooted pot that once belonged to Papa's mother, who had used it to feed the neighborhood. The result was always delicious, though if Mama's book was too exciting, the roast became soup. It didn't matter; both were delicious.

Mama's other specialty was baked apples. She would core them, fill them with raisins, and add a pat of butter and a touch of cinnamon. Then she set them squarely on pieces of white bread, which were buttered on both sides, and carefully placed them in the tiny oven of the Kachelofen, the tiled stove in the living room. The baking apples–fresh bread aroma would permeate our apartment and make it into a happy, safe place. Pot roast, soup, and baked apples are as precious as money in the bank.

My father had a way with Mama. When she seemed preoccupied and worried, he would waltz into her presence, take her hand, and sing "Che gelida manina," to which she always responded with a happy smile, showing the space between her front teeth, which Papa claimed was a sign of passion. Years later, when I found out that the song was Alfredo's aria to Mimi from Puccini's *La Boheme*, I became an instant opera lover.

These, then, are the personalities and ingredients of my "foreground." I use the word "are" because the ingredients are ever-present and the personalities tied to them live within me.

My Mother's Parents

It's good to bask in the sun and live close to one's grandparents.

—Yiddish proverb

My grandparents, Moritz and Helene Fabish, Opa and Oma, lived close by and spent a lot of time at our house. Oma didn't talk much, or even smile for that matter. She had arthritis and it hurt her to move. She was also losing her sight but loved to hand us bonbons with soft centers, which I hated. My brother ate everything fast. It took him one minute to crunch a bonbon and swallow it. I liked to let tastes linger and when Oma, giving me half a smile, popped one in my mouth, I would pretend to be pleased and rush to the toilet to spit it out. Could there be anything worse than biting into bonbons with soft centers?

Opa had opinions on everything—from Hitler, who was about to become chancellor, to how to bring up children, and even on growing radishes in bad times: in flower boxes, on the balcony. He was a living encyclopedia.

What I liked best was their yellow canary. She was called Goldie and sang all day long, until Oma would cover her with a white cloth and say sweetly "go to sleep little one."

One afternoon while sipping a cup of coffee and admiring the radishes that had sprouted in the window box, Opa expressed another of his opinions, this time about the need to give to community. I was half listening, but when he said he had contributed funds for the elephants in the zoo, I couldn't believe my ears and asked, "You mean you donated Lola?" She happened to be the lead elephant.

Opa was amused. "Well most of her," he said.

"What do you mean 'most of her'?"

"Let's say the two back legs and the body."

"How about the trunk?"

"Well," he mused, "throw in the trunk," as though it were a card game. He seemed to be enjoying our conversation.

The very next day, on the way home from school, I visited Lola, our family's elephant. I was so proud. When I saw people toss peanuts in her trunk, I thought to myself that if it weren't for my Opa, they wouldn't have Lola. I visited Lola almost every day, sometimes with my best friend Adelheid. She quickly got sick of these daily visits and spent the time going to mass instead, which her mother insisted on.

Thirty years later, long after the war, I visited Berlin and one of my visits was to the zoo. There was another Lola elephant, which I photographed and share with my students along with my story of a proud, little girl who never, ever, got tired of her grandfather's donation.

My Very Best Friend, Adelheid

True friends are a sure refuge.

—*Aristotle*

Best friends, true friends, are a necessity your whole life, whether you are young or old. Best friends listen to your secrets and worries and are always there to help you. You never need to tell them a lie because they are on your side and understand everything. You see them every day except when you go to far-away family reunions. The close ones they attend.

Adelheid was my very best friend. Our mothers met when they were carrying us in their respective stomachs. Adelheid believed that we had met in another life because we were so close and knew each other so well that we did not even have to talk. She lived close by. She called for me every day on the way to school. Our mothers were also friends. They shared recipes, books, and secrets. You could always tell when they talked secrets, because they stopped talking when we came into their presence and looked embarrassed.

Adelheid was an only child but, besides being her best friend, she called me her sister. Our specialty was to follow and carefully observe couples in love. We would dart behind a bench or tree if they looked back. Sometimes we would permit Bibi, my brother, to come along, but he had the habit of howling at the most inappropriate moments. We therefore avoided inviting him, but sometimes he just tagged along. "He's your brother," said my mother. "He's entitled." But then Adelheid and I never told her exactly what we were doing. We both loved Mama's older brother Adolf and Tante Hete, his bride. At family gatherings, we would watch them "like" each other. We walked Buffi, their terrier, whenever possible.

Adelheid was Catholic and celebrated Christmas. I enjoyed seeing her family's annual crèche: Mary, Joseph, Baby Jesus, the kings, and all the animals. Opa once stated that Christmas was the celebration of the birth of a Jewish baby. I thought that was very nice and gave our families something in common, but when I happened to mention it to Adelheid's grandmother, she was not amused and said I got my facts wrong. "How could Jesus be both Catholic and Jewish?" I didn't feel like checking with Opa because he was so sure of everything and I was not in a mood for a long explanation.

I did enjoy helping to decorate their Tannenbaum (fir tree) and sing "Oh Tannenbaum, Oh Tannenbaum, wie gruen sind deine Blaetter. . . ." We regularly received pink marzipan pigs for good luck, which Adelheid and I loved to eat together; we'd bite their heads off first and their tails next, and giggle.

Adelheid celebrated Hannukah with us and sang the hymn "Maoz Tzur" (Rock of Ages), which Papa particularly loved because it is about the miracle of survival of the Jewish people in yet another period of crisis. "You can't rely on miracles, but sometimes they do happen when you least expect them," he said. Mama gave us chocolate *gelt* (coins), which weren't nearly as much fun to eat as marzipan pigs. Mama's specialty, with the help of Tante Hans, Oma's sister who lived with us, was to prepare new annual outfits for our favorite dolls, my Angelika and Adelheid's Beate. We would parade our newly decked-out "children" around the courtyard and show them off to anyone looking in our direction.

Tante Hans was old but had young ideas. Once she told Adelheid and me about the pleasures of reading stories in bed before falling asleep. She suggested that we let a small piece of chocolate (like Hannukah *gelt*) melt slowly on each of our tongues while we read in bed. "It makes the reading oh so sweet." Mama objected, "You spoil your teeth that way." Tante Hans would wink and show us her teeth, which had received the chocolate treatment for seventy-seven years and showed only a little yellow stain here and there. Sometimes, I think, Tante Hans and Mama didn't like each other, but then again, often they did.

"It's never boring over at your house," said Adelheid. "Boring" is the major plague in childrens' lives.

Germany between the Wars

Following World War I, Germany, as the defeated nation, agreed to the Versailles Treaty, accepting blame for causing the war. As a result its people were forced to pay reparations (damages) to the Allies and to accept a democratic form of government called the Weimar Republic. For a while, most Germans, though unhappy, accepted these conditions, learning to live as citizens of a democracy and beginning to rebuild their country with financial help from the United States. But after the U.S. stock market crash in 1929, a worldwide economic depression began, putting a halt to Germany's recovery. Unemployment led to widespread misery, demoralization, and desperation, especially among young people. Political parties, each offering its own solutions to these problems, held patriotic rallies and parades, trying to win supporters. These often became violent.

Poverty, fear, disorder, and a lack of faith in the new form of government made the German people ripe for the ideas of Adolf Hitler and the Nazi Party. Hitler promised them jobs, discipline, and a renewed sense of German pride. And most of all, he placed the blame for all of Germany's problems—losing the war, corruption of the government, and destruction of the economy—in the hands of the Jewish people, making the solution to these problems simple: Rid Germany of the Jews and its problems would be solved.

The first Jews had settled in Germany during the time of the Roman Empire and their descendants had remained there for over a thousand years. Although anti-Semitism (prejudice against Jews) existed in Germany throughout this time, Jews had been accepted and treated as full citizens since 1870 and had become valuable members of their communities. In the 1920s, 600,000 Jewish people lived in Germany, about one percent of the population. They were doctors, lawyers, teachers, journalists, actors, writers, businessmen, and owners of shops and department stores, and they generally lived as average, middle-class citizens. During

World War I, 100,000 Jewish German soldiers served in the army, and 12,000 died for their country. By the time of the Great Depression, more than one out of three were unemployed, as were their fellow Christian Germans.

Most German Jews, like American Jews at the time, were not very religious, although Jewish culture and traditions were still important to them. Intermarriage was not uncommon. When Hitler began his campaign, the Jews of Germany were not only extremely surprised, but they also firmly believed that even if Hitler were to be elected, the German people—their friends and neighbors and family members—would vote him out of office very soon.

Adolf Hitler had been preparing to take over Germany since the end of World War I. He first attended a meeting of the German Workers' party as a spy, wishing to learn about its members and how the party could be used to overthrow the Weimar government. As a member, he changed the party's name to the National Socialist German Workers' Party (Nazis). Following a failed attempt to stage a coup, Hitler was jailed but served only one year of his sentence (many members of the judicial system were still very angry about being forced to accept the new democracy, and they did not want to see Hitler punished). While in prison, Hitler wrote Mein Kampf, *explaining his hope to take over Europe for Germany and to annihilate the Jewish people.*

By the time Hitler was released, conditions in Germany had worsened. By 1930, 6.4 million people had joined the Nazi Party. In 1933, a coalition with another party gave Hitler enough votes to become Chancellor of Germany. In addition, his "Brownshirts" or SA (stormtroopers), were holding torchlight parades and fighting battles against German Communist party members, the Nazis' primary opposition. On February 27, the Reichstag (parliament) building was burned to the ground.

Blaming the Communists, Hitler used this event to frighten those who did not support him into invoking Article 48 of the Constitution. This one clause made possible the death of democracy in Germany. It allowed the President to suspend civil liberties, such as freedom of speech, the press, and assembly, "for the protection of the people," and to impose the death penalty on anyone who "seriously disturbs the peace."

On March 23, having murdered or sent to Dachau the legislators who opposed him, Hitler succeeded in getting the Reichstag to pass the "Enabling Act," giving him the sole power to make the laws of Germany.

Adolf Hitler Becomes Chancellor of Germany

Why, man he doeth bestride the narrow world
Like a colossus, and we petty men
Walk under his huge legs and peep about
To find ourselves dishonorable graves.
—Shakespeare, Julius Caesar

The crowds in the streets are waiting to be led.
—Lenin

The crowds must be swept into the tremendous
stream of hypnotic intoxication.
—Adolf Hitler

January 1933

On January 30, 1933, Hitler legitimately assumed power in Germany and started the process of sentencing to horrible deaths millions of men, women, and children, including six million Jews and every member of my family except me. His book *Mein Kampf* was a best seller. Had it been read, reflected upon, and discussed by the German people, perhaps life for me and millions of others would have been different. That's why I spend so much time reflecting and discussing important texts with my students.

The Fuehrer (leader), Adolf Hitler, was born in 1889, the same year as Berthold Nussbaum, my Papa. They both served in the infantry during the Great War (WWI), Hitler as lance corporal and Papa as second lieutenant, but now I sound like Opa, who liked to make these kinds of distinctions. On this particular night, for instance, Opa said, "Why, this Hitler can't even speak proper German. I assure all of you he won't last any longer than the other chancellors." Papa said, "Always expect the unexpected," while

Mama added, "He hates Jews and says so on every other page in *Mein Kampf.*" But we all knew Opa had lived the longest, studied history, and amassed a large sum of money, which definitely made him the expert.

January 30, certainly, was most unusual. "Such an outpouring of joy has never before been witnessed in the German capital," according to the announcer on our Blaupunkt radio, with its twinkling lights that seemed to twinkle more than ever. "Never before have the streets in Berlin been filled with so many, the old and the young marching side by side with the Brownshirts, the Fuehrer's army, to the beats of drums and the sounds of trumpets. Torches are lighting up the night sky as though it's day." We didn't need to be told, we could hear the sounds of the festivities coming through our front window, which overlooked Lessingstrasse, our street. Papa turned off the radio and pulled down the shades. Bibi asked whether he could play outside and was ignored. Tante Hans started to weep and knit furiously, Mama turned the pages of Stefan Zweig's latest book, *Beware of Pity,* and Opa talked about one of his friends, the Kaiser's doctor and a Jew, who had once operated on the Kaiser's shriveled arm and how ridiculous it was to assume that Hitler would hurt the Jews when they had done so much good for the German people. It was my turn to be ignored when I asked whether his friend had unshriveled the Kaiser's arm.

The night passed, another day dawned. Nothing seemed to have changed. There wasn't even any debris in the street outside our house. Maybe it was going to be alright. Maybe Hitler would be too busy finding jobs for the German people and have no time left over for making life miserable for Jews.

Remembering: The Great War (1914–1918)

> We stand firmly on the foundation of patriotic German ideology ... our bonds are inseparably united with the German fatherland!
> — *Founding statement of the Jewish National Student Federation, 1896*

> The Jews stabbed Germany in the back.
> — *Adolf Hitler, explaining Germany's defeat*

> ... we find men without mouths, without faces ... The sun goes down, night comes, the shells whine, life is at an end ... Still the little piece of convulsive earth in which we lie is held. We have yielded no more than a few hundred yards of it as a price to the enemy. . . .
> — *Erich Maria Remarque,* All Quiet on the Western Front

The Great War, as World War I was called, lasted four miserable years and ended in shattering defeat instead of, as was predicted, in a glorious victory for the Kaiser. The troops were supposed to have returned in time for Christmas—four short months after the fighting began. My father and his four brothers fought with great pride for the glory of their country. They knew the reason for the war was that a young Serb with the strange name of Gavrilo Princip had shot and killed the heir to the throne of Austria, Archduke Franz Ferdinand, and the woman he loved at a place called Sarajevo in Bosnia. How that event fitted into dying for the Kaiser, few people, including Papa, really understood, but for some reason dying for the Fatherland was the thing

The great war; my father is first on the left, middle row.

to do. Papa's older brother Adolf did just that. He died at the
battle of the Marne. Shortly before his death, he penned a letter
to his unborn son. "Should I fall in battle," he wrote, "be proud
my child. I will have died for the Kaiser in the service of our
country. There is no finer death." His twenty-two year old son,
Kurt, carried the letter in his wallet when he left for Colombia,
South America, to save himself from a horrible death in Auschwitz, which his father's former comrade, Adolf Hitler, was busy
arranging, and which ultimately engulfed his aging, widowed
mother. Years later, he showed me his father's letter, his only connection to his brave, proud father.

When Bibi or I would fuss or complain about the cold or some
other discomfort, Papa would take the opportunity to inform us
about the horrors of trench warfare, the stench of decaying bodies,
the mud, the rain, the cold—all for gaining a few yards of ground.
And how his "Kameraden" (comrades) did not complain. When
I argued that the comparison was not fair because we weren't at

war, he would laugh and agree. "You have a point," he said, giving me a big grin that suggested I had won this argument.

The "comrades" look happy in the photo taken at Toulouse, where they were prisoners of war. "We had left the trenches behind us, that was a gift from above," said Papa. Years later, we learned from Felix, the comrade holding the ax, that Papa had met a French girl who smuggled in some sausage, cheese, and wine, which Papa shared with him. I liked this story and would have liked to know how the French girl and Papa met. But I never asked. It did not seem fair to Mama, although Papa had not even met her then. It seemed so typical of Papa—making the best of every situation.

My First Big Lie

A truth that's told with bad intent
Beats all the lies you can invent.

—William Blake

When I use a word, Humpty Dumpty said . . .
It means just what I chose it to mean . . .

—Lewis Carroll

Spring 1933

This particular day started like any other. Adelheid and I were on our way home from school. We had just walked over the bridge that spans the River Spree when Adelheid said:

"There is a picnic in the Tiergarten on Sunday. Everybody is invited. There will be free hot dogs, ice cream, polka music. Evchen, we'll see love couples dance. Oh, I forgot, they are also giving out free flags."

"Flags, what flags?"

"Oh, you know, the red flags with the white center and the swastika."

I knew immediately something was wrong and had that queasy feeling when I asked at supper whether we could all go to the picnic. "What picnic?" asked Mama. I did my best to explain without going into details about the flag. Mama turned ashen and said, "Nazis have invitations plastered at every corner." Papa said one word, "No," without even a hint of a smile.

"Why?" I asked, although I sensed the answer.

"Because we are Jewish."

"What's that got to do with it?"

"We celebrate Hannukah," said Bibi, trying to be helpful. Everybody stopped eating, including Tante Hans who enjoyed eating more than anybody. I left the table and went to my room. What was I going to tell Adelheid?

The next morning on our way to school, she asked me if I was going to wear the pink dress with the blue polka dots or could she borrow it for the picnic. I swallowed hard and told her she could borrow it, but I couldn't come.

"Why not?" she wanted to know.

"Well," I said, "because Oma is going to have a family reunion and I must be there. Tante Hete and Uncle Adolf are bringing Buffi." I knew Adelheid would understand because we both loved Buffi, the terrier, and walked her whenever we had the opportunity.

On Sunday evening Adelheid came to visit. Oh, the picnic was fun, but she had missed me. There had been nobody to giggle with. And she was sorry about the mustard stain on my dress, which her mother had tried to remove without luck. "How is Buffi?" she asked. "Oh, Buffi is fine," I said quickly. "She's going to have a puppy." Adelheid was thrilled. "A puppy. Are you serious?" It occurred to me that one lie leads to another so easily.

Thank goodness Papa came in the room. "Tell us a Sherlock Holmes story, just one." I pleaded. And there we were once again like old times: Adelheid, Bibi, and me, sitting at Papa's feet, listening to the familiar tale of the great English detective who was always ready and willing to solve all mysteries. This one we knew well and therefore helped tell.

Papa: "We find ourselves once again in foggy London where the street lights give off an eerie glow and tricksters, cheats, and murderers creep along dark alleys. What do you think Holmes was wearing?"

Bibi: "His purple dressing gown."

Adelheid: "His favorite."

Papa: "What's he doing?"

Me: "Sitting quietly like a spider in the center of its net, ready to pounce,"

Adelheid: "On the skinny man with the hook nose and the poison snake in his pocket."

Bibi: "Let Papa tell the story."

And Papa did, keeping us riveted as usual. The stories were always exciting and scary and made me forget scary things happening outside.

What Is a Communist?

Anyone who stands in our way will be mown down.

—*Adolf Hitler*

Things fall apart; the center cannot hold;
Mere anarchy is loosed upon the world . . .

—*Yeats*

A friend is a true refuge.

—*Aristotle*

Early Spring 1934

What happened to Herr Eugen Huber-Schmidt, whom my friend Adelheid and I called Hubi, shook us both up. Hubi was a glazier who fixed windows and lived in a basement apartment with his little brown-and-white Dachshund called Mimi. She had long velvety ears that Adelheid and I loved to touch. Hubi was kind and never in a hurry. He let Mimi take as much time as she wanted to savor other dogs' behinds. He explained to us that this was a dog's ultimate pleasure. He gave us bits of putty, which, during our boring school sessions, we would shape endlessly into interesting forms including, of course, dogs. Hubi also gave us bonbons with hard centers, which we enjoyed while sculpting. At school there were about forty students in each class and Adelheid and I made sure we sat in the last row so that the teacher would not notice our subversive activities.

One morning in May, shortly before my seventh birthday, Hubi didn't appear on the street, something we could not understand because he always walked Mimi several times a day. Maybe he was sick and needed help? We asked his neighbor, Frau Schulz, who greeted us with tears in her eyes and told us that the police had beaten him and taken him away. Beaten Hubi? "Why?" we asked.

"Because he is a Communist," she said.

"What's a Communist?"

"Ask your parents."

"What happened to Mimi?"

That's when her tears turned to sobs. "Mimi barked and whimpered and they beat her, too." Her husband had taken Mimi away. We had heard enough. We walked away. Adelheid grabbed my hand and we both tried not to cry. I had heard the word "Communist" before but could not remember where. I began to feel surges of icy fear rising from the pit of my stomach. I knew that something awful and unfair had happened. It was comforting to be with my best friend.

A month later Hubi returned. He was bent, could hardly walk, and kept staring at the pavement. One eye was closed. His mouth had shrunk. His teeth were missing. He no longer recognized us. After a while we gave up trying to remind him. Why Hubi? He was such a good person who loved Mimi, his little dog who made us laugh, sniffing all the time. Why would anyone want to hurt them?

A Sweet Birthday Party

There could I marvel My Birthday away
But the weather turned around.

—Dylan Thomas

Instead of dirt and poison, we have chosen to fill our
hives with honey and wax, thus furnishing mankind
with the two noblest of things, which are sweetness
and light.

—Jonathan Swift

May 15, 1934

This is just a simple story of an ordinary birthday party, my
very last. My first cousin, Hans-Werner (my Aunt Friedel's son),
and I were both born in May, an event we celebrated together.
Hans-Werner was going to be twelve years old and I was turning
eight. In the following photo, Bibi is on my right and cousins Susi,
Leni, and Helmut are in the front row. Of course I wanted books
for presents. I loved books with colorful illustrations. Some I could
read, others Papa would read to me. Hans-Werner got a new bicycle, which thrilled him. It wasn't Bibi's birthday but he ordered
boxing gloves. Papa promised him a pair when he got older. Bibi
always wanted boxing gloves and to this day I wish he had gotten
a pair.

What I remember most is the book Hans-Werner gave me. It
was about bees. Hans-Werner happened to love bees; his other
grandfather was a beekeeper who spent a lot of time explaining
what he called the secret life of bees to him. It was a slim volume
featuring a bee hive, a sun rising or setting—I never knew
which—and bees of all sizes buzzing around that sun. Because I
secretly harbored a seven-year-old crush on Hans-Werner, I fell
for the book and to this day remember that bees have been around

My seventh birthday, 1934.

for millions of years and they all get along. Thousands of undeveloped female workers and several hundred male drones follow the queen bee who rules. The male drones get fat and the sun is most important in the production of honey. When I can't sleep, I drink a cup of hot milk with honey and think of the fat drones, the sun, and that happy birthday party.

Everyone except Susi (below me in the photo) disappeared into Hitler's inferno. This story is a way of remembering them. Remembering (*zachor* in Hebrew) is essential.

The Last Happy Summer

Summer afternoon—summer afternoon; to me those
have always been the two most beautiful words in the
English language.

—*Edith Wharton*

But thy eternal summer shall not fade.

—*Willam Shakespeare,* Sonnet 18

Summer 1934

Tante Hans used to say that to her the proof of God's existence
was that we could not see into the future, which meant that we
were free to fully enjoy precious moments in the here and now
without worrying. I often think about that when I look at my
collection of three photographs from that last summer spent at
Swienemuende on the Baltic Sea, where we used to spend each
summer. We are visibly relaxed and happy enjoying the beach.
Bibi and I are on the horse. Notice who sits in front. In the afternoons we often listened to the band play in the pavilion. I would
watch couples dance and imagine myself dancing in someone's
arms in the rosy future ahead.

I will always remember Mama's red dress with sprays of white
forget-me-nots and adorned by the white fox fur collar that she
loved and I hated. How could she wear a dead fox around her
neck, I once asked Papa, who spent an unusually long time an-
swering me. Finally he laughed out loud, disarming the answer.
"You know, foxes really enjoy being prominently displayed. It
gives them longer life." I laughed, too, and that was the end of
the enquiry.

Papa would join us in Swienemuende for the weekends. He
came out on the train on Friday afternoons and Mama would wear
the favorite red dress all day in anticipation. She wore flats in the

Me and my brother at the beach.

morning and heels in the afternoon to look pretty, I am sure. When he arrived, they would sit in the shade of the big beach basket, talking away. I didn't know then how important it was for me to see them happy together. When you are a child you think everything that happens is normal, and that everybody has happy parents and summers at the beach.

My mother and father enjoying their last vacation at the beach in Swienemuende, Baltic Sea, summer of 1934.

The German Jews Lose Their Jobs, Their Property, and Their Rights

By April of 1933, the Nazi government began to strip the Jewish Germans of their rights. All Jewish civil servants were dismissed, including state physicians, dentists, teachers, professors, judges, and lawyers. By 1937, all Jewish-owned businesses (small shops, department stores, factories, banks, etc.) had been confiscated and were being sold at bargain prices to non-Jews.

In 1935, the Nuremberg Race Laws eliminated the rest of the rights of Jewish citizens. Complex definitions of "Jewish" became law, but basically anyone with one Jewish grandparent was considered Jewish, even those who had been raised as Christians, including priests, nuns, and ministers.

Jews were barred from: marrying or dating non-Jews; working for non-Jews; flying the German flag; owning pets; riding on the tram; sitting on park benches not marked "Jews only"; attending movies, theaters, and concerts; using public swimming pools; visiting playgrounds and parks where non-Jews were present; and dining in restaurants.

Bad News

Master of the Universe, look down from your heaven
and take a good look at your world.

—*Jewish prayer*

Out-worn heart, in a time out-worn,
Come clear of the nets of wrong and right,
Laugh heart, again in the grey twilight.

—*Yeats*

May 1935

In May 1935 Papa lost his job as general manager of a comforter factory where he had worked for twenty-five years. The silky-to-the-touch coverlets stuffed with pure goose feathers were popular. Business had thrived because of Papa. He had an eye for color, shape, and, of course, comfort, and he was a good friend to all the employees. That's what it said in the reference the father of the owner wrote. Papa treasured the reference and kept it in his inside pocket to show to everybody, including Opa, who was impressed.

The firing was not altogether unexpected. The owner, Papa's good friend, had retired, and his son, an ardent Nazi, was now in charge. It took him two days to fire Papa. On Papa's last day at work, some of the employees brought him bags full of sausages and several containers of Camembert cheese imported from France, which everyone knew he loved. Papa would have more time at the beach, I suggested with my mouth full of "running" cheese. "We have to skip this year," said Papa. "There will be other years, I promise."

Soon we were to discover that my teacher, Herr Weise, was another good, courageous human being. Adelheid told me one day, toward the end of summer, that she had heard that when we return to school in the fall, Jewish children would have to sit in the last row. What should she do, Adelheid asked me. True, she said, we liked sitting in the last row together, having our private fun, but after all, she was not Jewish. I had not seen much of her since she had joined the League of German Girls (Bund Deutscher Maedchen; BDM). She loved going to meetings and told me on a few occasions how much fun they were. We were still talking but she started to inject bits of awful news, such as she had heard that Mama's favorite author Stefan Zweig's books were burned in a big fire, and that's when I knew for sure she had begun to hate me. I ran home and told Mama, who immediately went to see Herr Weise, our teacher. He assured her that as long as he was teaching, he would sit his students where he pleased. And that's what he did. He wore a tiny swastika in his lapel that you had to strain your eyes to see. School became a hateful place. We had to say "Heil Hitler" twenty times during the school day and Adelheid gave me dirty looks when she happened to look in my direction. At the end of each day, we all had to march out the front door in unison and stand with our right arm outstretched as we sang the old German anthem, "Deutschland, Deutschland Ueber Alles" (Germany, Germany Over All), and "Die Fahne Hoch" (Hold the Flag High), the new one. I wore a cape so that you couldn't tell that my arm shook.

At the end of the year, Mama and Papa decided to take Bibi and me out of the Bochumer Strasse School, and they enrolled me in a tiny Jewish school where eight of us sat around the table, always in sight of the teacher. This was very difficult for someone who was used to doing her own thing in the last row.

School Life

By this time, public schools, too, had become threatening places for Jewish children. Teachers bullied and humiliated Jewish students, sending them out of the room when teaching "racial science" and then measuring their heads or noses in front of the class to point out the differences between Jews and non-Jews (none could be identified). Jewish students had to sit in the back row, with one or two empty rows between them and the rest of the class. Beatings by other children were common, particularly as Nazi Youth Groups were formed and new school books were printed to indoctrinate young people with hateful propaganda.

All students were subjected to a Nazified curriculum, which included performing the "Heil Hitler" salute up to 150 times a day and learning that "democracy" was a form of government run by rich Jews, that girls are inferior to boys except in the area of homemaking, and that boys are born to die for the Fuehrer. The popular German antiwar novel and film, All Quiet on the Western Front, taught in many American schools today, was banned. In May of 1933, a nationwide book burning destroyed 20,000 books at hundreds of universities. Among the authors considered "unGerman" were Jack London, Ernest Hemingway, Albert Einstein, and Helen Keller.

Long before laws forced Jewish students out of the public schools, many parents enrolled their children elsewhere. In 1934, 58,000 children out of 70,000 were in public schools. By 1936, only 23,600 remained. The rest were in Jewish schools, taught by teachers and university professors who had been dismissed from their positions. On November 15, 1938, Jewish children were officially barred from all schools.

Concerning a Good Eraser and Heinrich Himmler's Underwear

Experience is the child of Thought, and Thought is the child of Action
We cannot learn men from books.
—*Benjamin Disraeli, British Prime Minister*

Most of you know what it means when five hundred or a thousand corpses lie side by side ... To have stuck it out and at the same time remained decent fellows, that is what has made us hard. This is a page of glory in our history.
—*Heinrich Himmler in a speech to SS and Gestapo leaders in 1941*

Spring 1936

My new teacher, Fraeulein Vogelsang, had lost her job in the University of Berlin and started a small school of carefully selected students. The other students and I knew we were smart because we passed her examination. Mama was pleased that I could pass in spite of being "willful."

I hated this school, though not in the same way as the last one. I wasn't frightened, just bored and annoyed. Except for forty-five minutes for lunch, we were always on view. I couldn't scribble, chew candy, or even think my own thoughts. Opa was pleased that he had arranged this learning opportunity and was paying for tuition, which made it difficult to complain.

Miss Vogelsang believed in perfection and we did a lot of drills and rewrites. One particular day, she asked us to write from memory one of Heinrich Heine's lengthy poems and to be sure to include every comma and apostrophe. I omitted only one comma and Miss Vogelsang wrote "good" across the top of my paper.

I felt "good" was good enough for me so I erased her comment and handed in my "revision."

All hell broke loose. She phoned my parents and complained about my dishonest streak. Mama was upset and asked me why I couldn't do the assignment. "It would have taken you all of ten minutes." Papa smiled and said, "Evchen, if you want to do this sort of thing, you must get an excellent eraser."

He always understood, and what's more, he persuaded Mama and Opa to let me switch schools. I was then sent to the Lachmannschule in Gruenewald, where much of the instruction was done outside, under trees. I read more books there than I ever had and made lots of friends.

The Lachmannschule belonged to Fraulein Dr. Lachmann, also a former teacher, and it was located next door to the private villa of Heinrich Himmler, former chicken farmer and present chief of the SS (Schutzstaffel, protection squads), which, I would discover a few years later, controlled all the killing operations. Being busy, Himmler was probably never at home, but "his" underwear (to my mind) fluttered in the breeze. They were just like Papa's—to me a good sign. Besides, somebody in his villa would throw our misdirected balls back over the wall each day—another good sign. I kept working on a remedy for the troubles all around us, and I decided to personally invite Herr Himmler and Herr Hitler for Mama's pot roast and baked apples. They would enjoy the food and see that we were like everybody else.

My New Best Friend

You cannot tell the dancer from the dance.

—*Yeats*

A faithful friend is the medicine of life.

—Ecclesiastes

Summer 1936

The grandparents of my new best friend, Ruth Vera Pelz, had escaped the pogroms in Poland and settled in the Scheunenviertel in Berlin around the turn of the century. Ruth's mother was widowed and made a living as a seamstress. She specialized in sewing collars on shirts and dresses—at least a hundred a day to put food on the table, she would say. Yet, she still found time to outfit Ruth and me with tutus and satin bows.

The noise of the sewing machine blended perfectly with the heavenly sounds flowing from the ancient record player and it inspired Ruth to create a ballet in three parts entitled," Birth, Family, Death." In the first part Ruth unfolded and emerged from an imaginary womb to the music of "Weisst Du wie viel Sterne stehen"; next, she waltzed back and forth, with imaginary brothers and sisters, to the strains of the "Blue Danube"; and finally, she became the dying swan in Tchaikovsky's *Swan Lake*. My part was to shadow her movements and help her die. The finale consisted of both of us slowly returning to the seeds we once were.

The day Ruth's brother took the following photo, we were practicing taking bows in preparation for our performance the following Sunday evening. Later that day, sitting on the stoop of my house and totally absorbed in making final arrangements, we failed to notice Adelheid and two of her friends, in full uniform, stop right in front of us. Adelheid counted "One, two, three," and

Ruth, the ballerina.

the three girls spat at us in unison, screamed "Saujuden" (sow Jews), and then ran off. Ruth and I held on to each other just as Adelheid and I had once done when we found out what had happened to Hubi and Mimi.

Papa Disappears

You can laugh and feel like crying. But when you laugh, you make others laugh. And suddenly there is hope.

—*Berthold Nussbaum*

Even in laughter the heart is sorrowful.

—Proverbs 14:13

Fall 1937

On the Sunday of our planned ballet performance Papa disappeared. He had left his brother Max, who was making arrangements to leave for Shanghai via Italy, and was on his way home. All I could think of was Hubi and what had happened to him (he had since died). Mama sat by the window till it got dark. I could hear her muffled sobs during the night. Bibi ran errands for tips and Tante Hans made soup. Opa came over, said nothing, and put some money on the table. Papa's "comrade" attorney Johann von Ledersteger, who also owned our apartment, promised Mama he would do all he could to locate Papa, whom he supposed had been in a round up. "Berthold," he said, "received the Iron Cross [just like the Fuehrer]—that should help."

I was devastated. My father, my best friend, was gone. I spent all my time praying to der liebe Gott who had delivered us from Egypt. After a week of no news, I decided to give the Jewish God a rest and try Adelheid's Catholic God. I had noticed that there was a lot of kneeling in that religion and was willing to do my part to impress a busy God.

Winter arrived early that year and it was very cold in the former dining room where I slept on the couch because Mama had sold all the furniture and other treasures for much needed money.

Once I was totally warm and cozy, I would leap from under

my covers to the window, open it wide, and take deep breaths of the cold air. Then I would get on my knees, and pray. "Please Almighty Catholic God! Bring my Papa home because he is a very good man!" I was sure that the colder it got and the more the wind blew, the more effective my prayers would be. To further impress this unfamiliar God, I added ten minutes each night for endurance. I started to cough and my knees got sore. The more it hurt the better, I felt. I wanted "Someone Up There" to take notice.

After ten long weeks, Papa returned with his belongings in a cardboard box tied with string. I was positive it was due to my efforts and those of the Catholic God. Attorney Ledersteger was just a helper in the scheme of things. Everybody was there to greet him. Oma, Opa, and friends all listened intently to what had happened to him in the Moabit prison. "The food was terrible: watery soup and stale bread. But we had cards, played Skat, and told funny stories." It sounded like a vacation in Switzerland. We had done all the suffering, or so it seemed. That night when Papa once again sat on my bed, I challenged him and came straight to the point. "We missed you. We were afraid. Mama cried all night. I suffered too." I was a little vague as to how I had suffered. Papa was silent. "Didn't you miss us? Weren't you sad? How could you enjoy yourself like you said you did?"

After a long silence, Papa said, "Evchen, this might be difficult for you to understand, but it is possible to play cards, tell jokes, laugh, and be frightened all at the same time. You laugh and feel like crying. But when you laugh, you make others laugh. And suddenly there is hope. You feel the energy of laughter and friendship. And most important, you become the leader. You stand tall. And you know what, you will make a dent in setting things right. It's your form of resistance. Sorrow, outrage, infinite sadness, yes, tears, too, are ever present, but you are in charge, in charge of your laughter and your sorrow. Remember that always." And he tucked me in tighter than usual and left the door ajar so that I could see the light in the living room.

Crystal Night

On October 28, 1938, all Polish Jews living in Germany, such as Eve's friend Ruth, were expelled. From 1880 through the 1920s, many had emigrated from Poland to escape the pogroms (violent, anti-Semitic persecution encouraged by the government). Now, although they were being told that they must return to their "homeland," the Polish government refused to allow them in. They ended up living in squalid conditions in a "no-man's land," between Poland and Germany.

A young Jew living in Paris, Herschel Grynszpan, became so distraught over the expulsion of his parents from Germany that he barged into the German embassy and shot the first official he saw. Paul Goebbels, the German Minister of Propaganda, decided to use this incident as an excuse to persecute Germany's remaining Jews in a nationwide pogrom. During the night of November 9, 1938, 7,500 Jewish businesses were destroyed, and 1,000 synagogues were burned to the ground. That night, called Crystal Night because of all the broken glass, Nazi officials arrested 20,000 Jewish men, herded them into concentration camps, and held them for ransom. Many were beaten to death. The ashes of the dead were sent home in boxes to families able to pay for them.

In addition to this violence, the Jewish community was fined a $400 million penalty for the embassy official's death and the damage done to their own property.

Kristallnacht (Crystal Night)

I would not wish to be a Jew in Germany.
—*Hermann Goering, just after* Kristallnacht

What a new face courage puts on everything.
—*Ralph Waldo Emerson*

November 9, 1938

Glass shattered, synagogues burned, Torah scrolls became toilet paper, heads were bashed, and concentration camp Buchenwald overflowed with hapless victims, many of whom would not survive. Nazi troopers sang.

We arrived at school early on November 9 and were immediately sent home. From the S-Bahn we saw wrecked stores and the smoldering ruins of Berlin's finest temple, at the Fasanenstrasse, cordoned off by the police and firemen who made sure that the flames would not spread to nearby buildings. Passersby stood and stared.

That night, we stood together in the dark at the front window, watching the smoke rise from our Levitzovstrasse synagogue and listening to the noise in the street, punctuated by screams. Tante Hans's hand started shaking uncontrollably. I caught it and held it tight. She had always done for others. What was wrong with the world?

Suddenly the doorbell rang. Mama whispered, "Berthold, please, don't open. The Gestapo." Papa said, "It might be someone looking for shelter." And before Mama could respond, he was already by the door. Seconds later, he accompanied a trembling young man who whispered, "They're after me, please help. I read your name [Nussbaum] on the door."

"Sit down and relax," said Papa and he fetched the French

brandy reserved for special occasions. By the light of the street lamp shining in through the window, he poured some into a glass and added a lump of sugar. The young man sipped the drink very slowly and stopped shaking. He told us his name was Josef and asked how he might make an exit through the back alleys. Papa explained and had him repeat the instruction. After finishing the last drop, Josef was prepared to leave, in much improved spirits. "Maybe we'll meet again in happier days." Maybe.

He thanked Papa and clasped his hand. We all felt happier. We had had a respite from the horrible happenings in the night. The bluish-white light from the street lamp continued to shine on us— our little group huddled together waiting for the storm to subside.

The next morning the owner of the laundry offered to do our wash for free. "This is not our Germany," she said. Attorney Ledersteger, our landlord, visited and assured Papa that we could stay in his apartment as long as we wished, but the Nazi family who had moved in across from us jeered and said "Heil Hitler" every time we went by. The Lachmannschule closed; Himmler had found it an embarrassment.

Papa put on a pair of walking shoes and went from embassy to embassy trying to save his two children. He got up in the middle of the night so he could be first in line.

The Evian Conference

The events of Crystal Night were reported in newspapers all over the world, shocking many. In July 1939, President Franklin Roosevelt called for a meeting in Evian, France to discuss the problem of finding a safe home for Jewish refugees from the Nazis. Representatives from thirty-two countries attended. However, with the exception of the Dominican Republic, which offered 100,000 spaces, no country—not even the United States of America—was willing to take in more Jews.

Although the U.S. did promise to accept as many Jewish immigrants as its quota system allowed, even that did not happen. The rules for gaining entrance into the United States were often impossible to follow. For example, not only did one need to prove he had a job in the United States or a sponsor who would make sure he would not be a burden on the economy (Hitler's government would not let Jews leave with much more than the clothing they wore), one also had to have a "certificate of good conduct" from the local police, which in this case was the Gestapo. In addition, one had to produce all the necessary documents to the German authorities at the same time (sponsor, visa, exit permit, train, and boat tickets) and by a specified deadline. In the end, the United States took in 400,000 fewer Jews than its quota allowed.

At one point, Hitler offered to put Jews on luxury liners and send them anywhere. Holland and Denmark provided some room, Shanghai took in 14,000, and by the end of the war the countries of Latin America provided refuge for 80,000 German and Austrian Jews.

Adelheid Leaves My Life

If you have tears, prepare to shed them now . . .
                                              —*William Shakespeare*

I swear absolute allegiance to our Fuehrer . . .
                                      —*BDM Swearing in Ceremony*

Winter 1938

We had survived Crystal Night. Papa was in line at the U.S. embassy. Mama was visiting Oma, who could not stop weeping—two of her three sons had left Germany; would she ever see them again? Tante Hans was exhausted and slept. I was alone when the doorbell rang. Adelheid, in full uniform, stood outside. The week before, she and her friends had spat at me. Maybe she was sorry after seeing the horrors of the night. My illusion passed quickly. Without a greeting of any kind, she demanded that I hand over all the photos taken of us together since we were babies. I was unable to move.

"You know where they are, hurry up," she said. When I still did not move, she added, "They are in that cigar box in the bottom draw of your commode, in case you forgot." Was it my imagination or was she sneering? "Get them or I will." That did it. I ran to my room while she stayed at the door. A minute later I came back with the cigar box in which I kept my photos and spilled the contents on the floor. Photos of Adelheid and me as babies mixed in with those of my family greeted us, smiling. There was one of our first day of school, each of us carrying one of those large, decorated cones filled with goodies and licking chocolate lollipops. There was even one of us petting Mimi, Hubi's dachshund. Adelheid knelt down, tore the photos into many pieces, spilled them on the floor, and yelled, "You people are like rats," and left running.

I picked up the bits of photos, put them back into the cigar box, and locked myself in my room and cried until I had no tears left. Her words had devastated me. We had been best friends ever since we were babies. What happened? We were rats? How can you change from best friend to a rat? These questions have pre-occupied me for most of my life. On this day they came into sharp focus.

I told Mama I had a bad headache when she returned. Papa knew something terrible had happened and asked me about it during our nightly conversation.

"How could she do this?"

Papa thought for a moment, as though he, too, could not believe it. "It's certainly amazing given that you, as well as our families, were best friends all those years." He stopped. I thought I saw tears in his eyes. Then he concluded, "But I promise you the day will come when this will haunt Adelheid and she will ask you for forgiveness." Papa always knew the right, good words. He tucked me in, even though I was almost thirteen years old, and I fell asleep without any trouble.

I never had the opportunity to find out what Adelheid felt after the war. She left my life that day.

Part II

Holding On

The Kindertransport

One country responded, in a unique and positive way to the events of Crystal Night. A group of prominent Jews from England decided to visit Neville Chamberlain, their Prime Minister, and ask for temporary refuge for German and Austrian children who were suffering under Nazi rule. Their intention was to provide them with a haven until the Nazis were out of office, and they hoped that the United States would follow their lead.

Early in 1939, two members of Congress, Senator Robert Wagner (NY) and Representative Edith N. Rogers (MA), proposed the Child Refugee Bill, which would allow for 20,000 children. Groups of American Quakers were willing to deal with the arrangements for transportation and placement. Within one day of the announcement of the idea, 4,000 families of all faiths volunteered to take the children. Many religious groups supported the bill, as did First Lady Eleanor Roosevelt, but her husband ignored it. The bill was never even voted on. There were too many opponents, from anti-Semitic groups fearful of Jews—even children—to patriotic societies such as the Daughters of the American Revolution (DAR), the Veterans of Foreign Wars (VFW), and the American Legion, who supported a bill to stop all immigration.

However, members of the British cabinet agreed to accept 10,000 unaccompanied children. A group of Quakers, led by Bertha Bracey, and Christian members of Inter-Aid formed the Movement for the Care of Children from Germany, and immediately began to search for homes for the children and money. (The government required a guarantee of £50, $1,500 today, so that in case the children did not return home, they would not cost the British government anything.)

Also needed was transportation to England, to homes, hostels, or camps, and money to finance all this. On November 25, 1938, the BBC broadcast an appeal for foster homes and almost immediately received 500 offers, and many volunteers to check the homes for respectability.

On December 8, former Prime Minister Stanley Earl Baldwin went on the radio to plea for more help. "I ask you to come to the aid of victims not of any catastrophe in the natural world, nor of flood, nor of famine but of an explosion of man's inhumanity to man" (The Kindertransport Souvenir Reunion Booklet, 1989). *Free shoes came from the famous Marks & Spenser department store and a manor hall was donated by Baron James de Rothschild. Castles, farms, and other homes were donated, as was £500,000 by the British people.*

Jewish groups volunteered to guarantee the £50 for each child and to help find them homes. In Germany, Jewish organizations made lists of children under seventeen, identifying the most urgent cases: Polish children being deported, orphans whose parents were in concentration camps or dead, and teenagers in danger of arrest or already in camps.

Two young men, Nicholas Winton, 29, an English stockbroker, and Norbert Wollheim, 25, were mainly responsible for the saving of these 10,000 children. Winton had visited the refugee camps created in Czechoslovakia after Hitler had taken the Sudetenland (a section of the country inhabited mostly by Germans) and was shocked by what he saw. He appointed himself secretary of the "Children's Section" of the "British Committee for Refugees from Czechoslovakia," created some official-looking stationery, had all of the children in the camps photographed, and sent out a plea to have them rescued. Six hundred of the 6,000 children on his list were saved. (149) When the war broke out, 250 children were on a train in Prague, waiting to depart to safety. Had they left one day earlier, they would have been saved. Said Winton, "Not a single one of those children was heard of again, which is an awful feeling, isn't it?" (182)

Wollheim escorted the children coming from Germany, but each time he had to return to Germany, knowing that the operation would be cancelled if he did not. In 1943, Wollheim, his wife, and their three-year-old son were deported to Auschwitz. Only he, out of 70 family members, survived. (282)

Parents who had registered their children for the Kindertransport were sent dates and departure information, sometimes with only a few days notice. The stress of packing (trying to cram forbidden valuables into suitcases after they had been searched and sealed by the Gestapo—one girl pushed her stamp collection into her suitcase one stamp at a time) and collecting photographs of loved ones as keepsakes and as enticements to strangers to take in their families, while trying to remain hopeful about the future, left children angry, sad, and frightened. Some, too young to understand what was happening, felt rejected by their parents; others felt excited about the journey their parents had told them about.

One cannot even imagine what the parents of these children were going through. Years later one survivor, Charlotte Levy, tried to recall her emotions. "The degree of despair to which you can be driven is best revealed by this reversal of one's normal feelings and principles. To feel happiness about what? About being able to send one's little boy of 9 away to a foreign country whose language he does not speak, to people one does not know oneself, not sure if one will ever see home again." (Harris and Oppenheimer, 2000, 82)

On December 1, 1938, the first train from Berlin departed. German officials at the Dutch border also checked the children's luggage, brutally checking for forbidden items. The children were accompanied by adults who were required to return to Germany or the program would be cancelled. In March trains began leaving from Prague.

When they arrived in England some children had already been assigned homes and were met by their families or sent to them by train, while others were held in hostels or summer camp facilities, waiting to be chosen. Unfortunately, the camps had no heat and no way to provide schooling or much recreation in the winter. Brothers and sisters were usually separated because few homes had the resources to take in more than one child. There were loving families with children ready to take in new siblings, as well as families who merely wanted maids, or even a wife for their son. Occasionally conditions were even worse, and children were abused. Older teenagers were frequently rejected and stayed in hostels until they turned 16.

For all the children, the experience was new and frightening. Because there were not nearly enough offers from Jewish homes, most lived with Christians who tended to ignore the children's religious heritage. Some

Kinder arriving in Southampton, England.

children, especially the youngest, were given a new name, identity, and religion.

At first letters arrived from home, often with cheerful greetings and advice, as well as pleas for help in finding homes for siblings and parents. In response, the children wrote letters, knocked on doors, and pleaded with relatives to rescue their loved ones. But by September 1939, mail

A young girl waiting for her foster family.

was sent only through Red Cross workers—and these letters were short and upsetting, carrying news of deportations and arrests. By 1942, so-called evacuations to the East were well under way, and many people knew this was most likely a death sentence. At the war's end, the children—and by this time a number of them were young adults—learned that nearly all of their parents had been murdered.

After the war, the children, even many of those not yet sixteen, were on their own. Only a few reunited with their parents, who had suffered unbearable trauma and often seemed like virtual strangers. Unlike today, there was no one to provide counseling—no trauma centers, mental health agencies, doctors or psychologists—to help anyone recover from their devastating experiences. The children had lost their families, their possessions, their homes. Some even lost the ability to speak their native language. They were expected to forget their past and move on, alone. It was not until June 1989—the first Kindertransport reunion—that they were able to talk to others who understood what had happened to them.

Refugee

Good-bye, proud world! . . .
Thou art not my friend, and I am not thine.
                                    —*Ralph Waldo Emerson*

. . . the grief that does not speak
Whispers the o'er-fraught heart, and bid its break
                          —*William Shakespeare,* Macbeth

July 1939

Loneliness enveloped me that first night at Studley. I could hardly breathe. "Why?" I kept asking der liebe Gott. "It's not fair." And surely God knew it wasn't fair. Just in case He was busy or not listening, I started to build a case against the "unfairness." I began recording the events of my life from that day on.

July 1, 1939

It's only six hours since I walked off the plank of the *SS Washington*, recognized Uncle and Auntie from the photo they sent, and yearned to return home. They waved to me but did not look happy to see me. They did not even smile. In the train to Ipswich I tried out my 42 words of English in various combinations: How are you? I am fine. My parents are fine. You have chickens and apples? They said "fine" and didn't ask any questions back. Maybe if I give them the apples I collected on the boat, they'd smile. We'd munch together. Their mouths would move. That's what I thought. But Auntie took one look at my spit-polished apple and said, "I can't eat apples. You see, Eva, I have false teeth," and she took her teeth out to show me. Uncle took the apple, examined it carefully, took a bite, and stammered "These must be American apples. They have looks but no taste." He kept tapping his foot. Maybe that's what you have to do when you

The refugee between "Uncle" and "Auntie," feeling "untouched" and miserable in Foxhall, Ipswich, Suffolk, England.

stammer. He tried to return the apple but I was too busy blowing my nose so that they wouldn't notice my tears and I pretended to look out of the window.

It's eight o'clock. I have been in my bedroom for two hours. I thought they might come up and say good-night but no. When we got "home," Uncle showed me the orchard, the hens, and the two geese. Then he showed me the outhouse. He told me not to use too much sand because he has to empty the pail and doesn't like it heavy. I sat down and a fly flew up. I hated the feeling but it made me laugh. After tea and toast, they showed me my bedroom, told me to unpack, and get a good night's sleep. The sun is still up. Am I not allowed to go downstairs? I unpacked and mended a tear in my blouse. Would Mama ever be surprised. Mama, I am writing in the diary you gave me. There is no running water. To wash, there is a jug, a basin, and a pail underneath the stand where I am supposed to empty the slops from washing and the contents of the potty underneath the bed. The potty is decorated with roses, so is the jug, so is the basin, so is the picture above my bed. I put the suitcase with my doll Angelika and the photos underneath my bed, next to the potty. There is a fireplace with a mantle and dusty indentations. Twenty-four indentations. I took my crochet hook and made an X in the first thirteen—eleven months to go and we'll all be together. Was Uncle serious? I am only allowed to light the candle if absolutely necessary?

July 3, 1939

I feel like exploding. I hate it here. They don't understand. They don't want to know me or my family. I brought my photos down to show them after breakfast. They just looked at them fast and did not ask a single question. I'll never show them the photos again. Nothing, nothing works. It took me a while before I gave them their gifts that Mama had so carefully wrapped. Uncle tore it open and there were—surprise—Papa's cufflinks. *Oh lieber Gott.* Auntie unwrapped Mama's silver lace pin with the pearl in the center. She seemed to like the pin. Too bad. I would have liked it. It was Mama's favorite pin. Uncle gave the cufflinks back. He doesn't wear shirts with sleeves. The cufflinks are in my suitcase with the photos and Angelika. Papa will be surprised to get them back. Auntie said "thank you." That's all. She didn't examine the pin or say how beautiful it is. Uncle gave me the rules and made me repeat them: 1. Help Auntie. 2. Do the dishes and get water from the pump outside the kitchen door. 3. Uncle is in charge of collecting the eggs in the hen house. (I would have liked to do that.) 4. Bedtime is seven o'clock in the summer and six o'clock in the winter. 5. When I go to school, I am allowed a visit from one friend every two weeks. 6. No seconds for food. (I am always hungry.)

July 6, 1939

I keep crying. I will get bags under my eyes and will look old and ugly soon. What's good about crying is that it makes me fall asleep, but then, in the middle of the night I am wide awake, like now, and I write this diary in the dark. The moon and the stars light up the night sky. You can see the outline of trees. I recite Mama's favorite poem, by Goethe.

Ueber allen Gipfeln ist Ruh
In allen Wipfeln spuerest du kaum einen Hauch
Die Voeglein schlafen im Walde
Warte nur balde, ruhest du auch.

Above the treetops is peace
You can hardly feel the gentle breeze
birds are asleep in the woods
Just wait, soon, you too will rest.

July 12, 1939

I was allowed to plant a baby tree. I chose a little green pine tree with drooping branches. The tree looked lonely and lost. I planted "him" (der Baum) underneath my window so I can watch him grow.

July 15, 1939

I have been here for two weeks. Time goes so slowly. I wait for the postman every day. So far I haven't received one letter. Papa said he would write as soon as he got home. I have sent three, that's all because Uncle stammers, "That's enough. Stamps cost, my dear." Lately he calls me "my dear." He teaches me English words between nine and ten in the morning so I can keep up in school. It's hard to listen to him because he stammers. BUT I WANT TO LEARN. He also walks me for my "constitution," because I can't go in the outhouse on account of the flies. Every three days, I explode.

July 17, 1939

I hate it here and want to go home. I was happy in Berlin, in Nazi Germany. Yes I was frightened, but I was happy. Here I am not frightened but I am so unhappy, I spend most of my time crying in bed. If it weren't for the stars, the moon, my little tree, and knowing I will be together with everybody soon, I would want to die. I have NOT met a single person my age.

July 18, 1939

The postman waved three letters to me. They had all been opened by the German censor. Papa types the most, everyone else writes. They are so happy I am here. They received two of my letters. And give a thousand thanks to Uncle for teaching me English. I put the letters in my suitcase. There, I can always reach them when I can't sleep. Bibi sends me one page and one kiss. He saw Ruth. She misses me. I am so happy to have their letters and can't bear it at the same time.

July 25, 1939

Yesterday was the very worst day. We visited Uncle's cousin Mr. Green on Avondale Road in Ipswich and after that we walked through a big park called Christchurch. Everybody was having a good time. Dogs, children, grown-ups. They can walk on the grass here. And then I saw an ice cream man with his little cart. I pointed to him and said "Ice cream, please," but Uncle said something about ice cream being a luxury and I would have to get used to doing without luxuries. After all, he got rid of electricity. And that's that. I can't sleep. I look through the window: tears, stars, and my little tree merge. I pray *bitte, bitte lieber Gott*, bring us all together. I look out at the view bathed in hues of silver and white. There is so much space. The fields run into one another. Why, oh why, can't they just come over? We could live in a little nothing hut on the edge of that field near the big oak. We could have picnics just as we did in the Tiergarten. Nobody would notice. *Bitte, bitte Lieber Gott!*

August 3, 1939

I stole a sweet from the tin on the sideboard. I couldn't help it. Hope Auntie didn't count them. Sweets are luxuries that I can have only once in a while. A cat, a dog, a rooster are luxuries that we can never have. Uncle noticed I didn't close the back gate. I had to write 100 lines, "I must close the back gate." I got another letter. Did I try to find a home for Bibi, asks Papa. Uncle won't allow me to bother people. How can I tell Papa that?

August 15, 1939

They went off to a Peace Pledge meeting, here was my chance. I ran through the gate and the woods to Foxhall Road where the Goodings live to ask them about taking Bibi. They always ask me

My brother, Bibi.

about Bibi in Kesgrave Church. I go to church (Opa!) because it's better than dusting and they serve biscuits and tea after the service. Mrs. Gooding looked at Bibi's photo. "What a lovely looking young man," she said. "But we only have the one, Bobby, you know." "But they can play together, can't they, please?" She promised to think about it and I ran off to the Mansars who lived on the way home. Mrs. Mansar came to the door. She looked as though she had been crying. Before I even had a chance to ask, she whispered that Neil, her husband, was in the hospital with a heart attack. I said I was so sorry. I ran through the woods past the sanatorium. Uncle and Auntie were home and furious. Both talked at once. "We told you not to bother people. Write 500 lines: 'I shall never again bother people.' " Oh Papa, what do I do?

August 30, 1939

I bet Uncle and Auntie took me in to help them around the house and so they get into heaven. They always introduce me as the "German Jewish refugee child." I like to keep the treasures in my suitcase in a mess, so when I reach for something it is always a surprise. Angelika, my doll, is in charge. Sometimes I just hug her. Her (my) dress is wearing out from all the tears and the hugging.

Treasures in the suitcase kept under my bed.

September 1, 1939

We do not have a radio or a newspaper. "They are luxuries and bring bad news," says Uncle. The postman waved another letter and says he is worried about war. Ruth and her family have disappeared. Ruth??? War??? I am so afraid. I did not manage to find a place for Bibi. What's going to happen? Uncle says "Nothing. We'll keep going about our business." "A lot happened in Germany," I said. "You must leave some things to God, my dear," he stammers.

September 3, 1939

It's war! Where is Ruth? I write lines almost every day. I am naughty. I can't write anymore. My nose is running. I can't see. I am so lucky they aren't my parents. I bet they don't know how to make babies. I reach for my letters under the bed.

September 9, 1939

There was a German plane straying over East Anglia. I heard the sound of anti-aircraft fire. I wish they had hit the plane and the pilot had parachuted outside my window. I could have spoke German. Maybe he wouldn't have hated Jews.

September 15, 1939

In two days school starts. A friend. A friend. A friend. Bitte lieber Gott send me a friend. Some anonymous, generous lady is paying my tuition for a private girls' school called Ipswich Public Day School for Girls. I have to wear a uniform. The teachers are paying for them. You are supposed to have three dresses, in brown, yellow, and blue. Uncle (he makes all the decisions) has permitted me to have one. I chose the blue one. Mr. Green gave me a bicycle from his garage. I live four miles away from the school. I am ready. I have studied English on my own.

September 17, 1939

It's just awful what happened at recess. About five girls from my class stood in a semicircle facing me. "Is it true you are German?" said the tallest one. She looked cross. "Yes." What was

I going to say? "Where from in Germany?" "From Berlin. I was born in Hannover." "That's all Germany. Do you know we are at war with Germany?" I said nothing. I felt that lump in my throat and those tears welling up. "You must feel funny being our enemy," the girl said while the others stared at me. Then they left me by myself. What should I have said? How can you explain anything to people who don't want to know. I don't understand anything myself. The bell rang. Recess was over. As I was going in, a girl from the circle approached me. "I am Mary," she said. "This whole war must make you feel terrible." A friend, perhaps. Thank you lieber Gott.

September 18, 1939

I miss you so much Ruth. Where are you? I can't see to write. I HOPE YOU ARE ALL RIGHT. I LOVE YOU SO MUCH.

September 19, 1939

Mary eats lunch with me. So does her friend Wendy. I hate the cold cabbage sandwich Auntie gives me. I am the only one (except for two girls who have allergies) who does not get to eat a hot lunch. And it smells so good. I hate to take too much of Mary's lunch.

September 20, 1939

I AM HAPPY. I got a Red Cross message. They are all right and still hoping. . . . They send me kisses. Kisses! Haven't been touched since I arrived. Maybe they'll send me a real letter through Onkel Karl who lives in Switzerland.

October 4, 1939

"My brother is twelve years old today. I wish I could have sent him boxing gloves," I announced at breakfast. No response. Then I asked if I could have hot lunch [at school] like everybody else. I am always hungry. "Auntie will add another half sandwich," said Uncle. I held my breath and said, "I really don't like cooked cabbage sandwiches. They smell funny." "They are good for you," said Uncle, stammering more than ever.

Class photo. *Third row from top:* **1. Sad-looking Eva** (*5th from right*), **2. Mary Cadman, friend** (*4th from left*), **3. June Brown, friend** (*5th from left*).

October 10, 1939

Finally I got permission for Mary to visit me on her bicycle. She arrived with Wendy and another girl called June. Uncle was furious, he called me in the kitchen. "I gave you permission for one friend," he shouted. He forgot to give me lines to write. A blessing.

November 4, 1939

One letter arrived via Onkel Karl in Geneva. I wrote back immediately. I want everybody to know that Shakespeare is funny. I am the Second Witch in *Macbeth*. I like my lines: "I kill Swine, and I give thee wind." Mary is 'First Witch . . . a rat without a tail' and June is Lady Macbeth.

December 3, 1939

My first report card is good. "I appear happy," says the headmistress. Happy? The occasional Red Cross messages, the "stuff" in my suitcase, and Mary really likes me. Uncle paid for an extra Red Cross message to tell everybody. They will be happy.

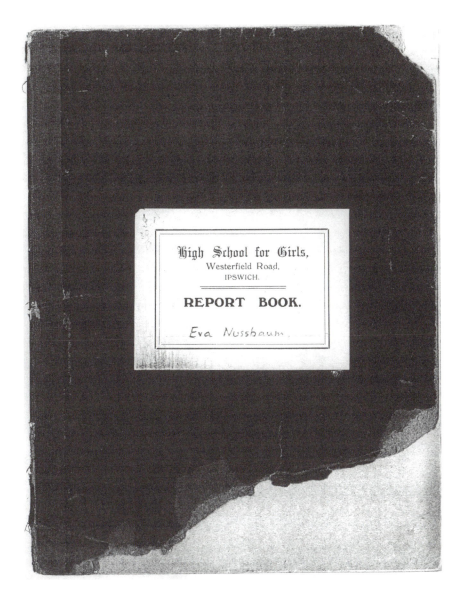

My report card, Autumn 1937.

Autumn Term, 1937

Age on 31st July last 13 years 2 months.

Average Age of Form on 31st July last 12 years 6 months.

SUBJECTS.	REMARKS.	
Scripture	Good. Eva has shown an intelligent interest in this subject.	S.M.
English	good, Eva is working very well and readily. and is rapidly overcoming her language difficulties.	G. de H.H
History	Fairly good. She has worked very well.	K.tn.tn.
Geography	Fairly good. She has worked hard.	K.A.B
French	She has worked hard and made really good progress.	S.J.L
German		
Latin ...	Fairly good.	S.M.
Arithmetic	⎫ Eva's progress is very satisfactory.	M.
Algebra	⎬	
Geometry	⎭	
Chemistry		
Physics	Fairly good.	M.V.
Biology		
Gymnastics	She has worked very hard and is making progress.	P.G.
Art	Very fair.	H.N
Needlework	Fairly good.	E.W.R
Piano ...		
Singing		
Elocution		

70

Form   L IV A.

Number in Form   18

Examination Standard   —

EXAMINATIONS:		
Percentage obtained	Highest Percentage Awarded	
		EXTERNAL EXAMINATIONS—

ATTENDANCE—

Absent   —   times.

Late   —   times.

GENERAL REPORT—

Eva has made a most satisfactory beginning. She appears happy in her surroundings and has worked well.

S. Midgley   Form Mistress.

Louisa E. Leaf   Head Mistress.

Next Term begins   Wednesday, January 17th

and ends   Thursday, April 4th

Half Term   Tuesday, February 27th

Holiday(s)   Monday, February 26th
March 22nd (Good Friday)
March 25th (Easter Monday)

71

Christmas Holidays 1939

I hate holidays. It's gloomy, gloomy and COLD. There's no music. There is a piano. Uncle plays and Auntie sings "Cherry Ripe ..." He won't teach me to play the piano, even though I begged him.

Christmas Day 1939

It's the holiest day for Christians. I asked for a hot water bottle so I could hug it at night and wash with the warm water in the morning. But no, I got big booties for my feet.

May 15, 1940

I am fourteen today. Last year at this time I was HOME. I hate it here. Nothing has changed. Occasionally I get a letter via Geneva. Mama sends a poem. Papa tells me he, too, had chilblains in the army and they pass. (I told him I had chilblains on my toes and one little finger.) I love them so much. Uncle wrote to Onkel Herbert in New York—could I go there? He hates me too. Of course, I can't, don't have a visa.

September 12, 1941

School has started. I have no energy. Yvonne Kenney, a girl who lives in a big villa, offered to have me live with her and her family. Everybody knows about my cabbage sandwiches and my one dress. But Uncle says either I live with them or he'll take me out of school and send me somewhere else.

January 6, 1942

Today is Tuesday and the first day back at school. Miss Neal and staff gave me a belated Christmas present: a tennis racket, tennis balls, and an outfit in time for the tennis season. Would I be able to take the gifts home even though it was drizzling? Would I ever! I am the only person in school who doesn't play tennis. I AM SO HAPPY.

January 9, 1942

Today I returned the racket, balls, and outfit. Uncle says NO and he is my legal guardian. He went to see Miss Neal yesterday and gave her three reasons and told them to me before supper:

1. He has noticed I love tennis more than God.
2. In my position in life, he does not expect me to play tennis because it's an upper class sport. And it is wrong to give me tastes and desires "unfitting to my circumstances."
3. Miss Neal should have asked him first.

I said nothing. I went to bed.

February 10, 1942

I haven't had a Red Cross message or letter for so long. I can't concentrate. All I want is to go to bed and lie there till my parents come and get me. Why must I be "here" and they "there"?

February 13, 1942

Last night I pushed my bed all the way against the window. Auntie heard the noise and came in. She was annoyed and said I was supposed to be sleeping. "From now on," she said, "you are to pull the shade down when you go upstairs." My bed is like a coffin now. I tried so hard. Lieber Gott help me.

This was my last entry. Pulling the shade down stopped me from functioning. I felt alone, isolated, and abandoned. I continued getting up, going to school, but I lost interest. There were no letters, no messages, no stars, no hope. I stopped eating and writing in my diary. There was no point.

In the middle of the spring of 1942, Auntie and Uncle accompanied me to Ipswich Station. I was going to become a nursery helper to evacuated children from London, in a place called Hertford. Uncle gave me some written instructions:

1. All you have to worry about is your constipation. Drink a glass of hot water.
2. Write us, if you have time.
3. In two months, you will be sixteen and an enemy alien. Be-

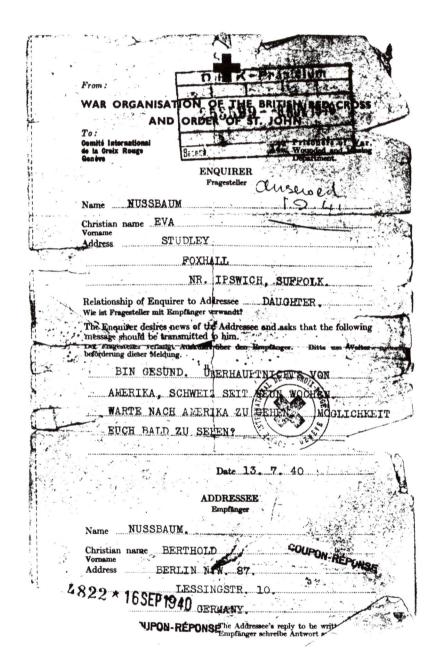

My last Red Cross message: Am healthy. No news from Switzerland for nine weeks. Waiting to go to America. Possible to see you soon?

cause we live near Martlesham Airbase you can no longer visit us.

4. Save your money. You must become independent. You cannot expect us to help you.

And finally, Good-bye, take care of yourself. Maybe we can arrange to meet you outside of the area. Signed: George and Florence Rattenbury.

It took several years, but there came a day when I realized that George and Florence Rattenbury, who had heard about the plight of Jewish children and decided to become temporary guardians to an "endangered child," chose me and saved my life.

Part III

Reaching Out

Enemy Aliens

Once the war began the situation of the kinder in England also changed. Those over fifteen were now considered enemy aliens and were no longer allowed to live in militarily sensitive parts of the country. One thousand were held in camps, 6,000 were sent to Canada or Australia, and another 1,000 teenagers became Allied soldiers. Younger children continued with their education until they turned 16, and then were given menial jobs or unskilled labor. After the war, those who could continued with their education, many eventually earning college degrees.

Nursery Helper

Feel the dignity of a child. Do not feel superior to him.
—*Robert Henri*

Those are blessed, who have the heart of a child.
—*Anonymous*

And with a joy that is almost pain
And among the dreams of the days that were,
I find my lost youth again . . .
—*Longfellow*

Spring 1942

I ate my cabbage sandwich on the train to Hertford, munched on my freckled apple. Both tasted good.

I was on my own.

I had survived.

Miss Tilton, the director of Balls Park Residential Nursery School, under the auspices of the London County Council, was waiting for me at Hertford Station. "Ever so glad to meet you Eva. We need your help so badly." She shook my hand and hugged me, and insisted on carrying my "treasure chest" suitcase. "It's ever so heavy," she said. "What have you in there, bricks?"

On the bus to the residence, she explained there were sixty-seven children between three and six to care for. Some had dads fighting in the war, some mums working in munitions, some were orphans, a few had been bombed and needed extra loving. "What's good about the war is that it brings us together and willing to help one another. Take where we are: Balls Park Estate is on loan from Lady and Lord X. The children are from London's impoverished East End," she explained.

After a quick lunch, Miss Tilton handed me a netted bag of

Working permits for "enemy alien" Eva Nussbaum; note that previous nationality is "nil."

multicolored building blocks and led me to a large room into which emerged an elderly lady surrounded by five noisy children. "Eva, meet Mrs. Gerrety, our splendid cook who helps us keep body and soul together. Eva is our new helper," she stated. "She is ready, eager, and willing, aren't you my dear? I do have to run," she said, all in one breath.

"Am I ever glad you are here, Miss Eva. You see I have to get on with tonight's stew. To get the full flavor you need to cook beans ever so long. You like beans?"

"I love beans. I could eat them all the time."

I was glad somebody had actually asked me a question and waited for an answer. Mrs. Gerrety reached in her pockets and put two butterscotch sweets in my hand so the children wouldn't notice. "Got to go," she said. "Now be good girls and boys for Miss Eva," and off she went, only to return a minute later. "Dear me," she said, "I forgot to introduce you to the children." And that's how I met Kevin, Annie, Beth, Billy, and Maureen, my charges.

The children simply stared. Ten pairs of eyes followed my every move. What was I supposed to do? The blocks, I decided, that's what. I opened up the bag, dumped them on the floor, and started playing. The children, all except Kevin, moved closer.

Playing with blocks was not part of my recent experience but I managed to line up two sets facing each other. Could be a road or maybe a canal? A canal, that's what I was building, because I could place a tugboat square in the middle. I looked up at the children with great satisfaction.

"What's that?" asked Beth. She had long braids. I loved braids and looked forward to styling them.

"A tugboat in a canal."

"What's a canal?" Beth asked picking at a pimple on her nose. I had no idea what to do about her picking at the pimple or how to explain the canal. Billy came to the rescue. "That's silly," he said, helping himself to the large blocks and building another tugboat, which he put next to a single row of blocks. "Tugboats ain't in canals, they're out at sea." I immediately widened my canal and explained that this was a special canal and a special tugboat.

A big tanker needs to be towed in. Who would like to help? "I'll help," screamed Annie and Beth together. Couldn't they have screamed a little less, I thought. I was new at the job and a little nervous. Maureen helped herself to the remaining blocks and announced, "I am making a huge tanker, with lots of little tugboats all around." Annie helped her set the chimneys while Beth watched.

I leaned back and relaxed. Mama should see me now. I had a way with children, just like Papa. But all of a sudden, Kevin, who had been observing me from some distance, introduced himself in a novel way. He charged forward, stopped suddenly, removed his left eye, and threw it in my direction, toppling one of the chimneys on the big tanker. I was left staring at his eye socket and froze. Maureen, whose tanker it was, picked up the eye, turned to me, and said "Don't take any notice of him. His eye got bombed. He does that all the time." Then she handed the bombed eye back to Kevin and commanded him to pop it back in and to stop being silly. I thanked Maureen and der liebe Gott in that order. Maureen, almost five, became my best friend. She and I would walk two miles to an ice cream parlor every other Sunday afternoon when I was off. We would "lick and look" at the world and try a variety of exploits such as picking cherries in late summer. Then each of us took turns spitting the pits as far as possible and checked carefully who won.

Two weeks' pay resulted in my first purchase: a hot water bottle. I have never been without one since, and I never, ever go to sleep with the blinds drawn.

Recipe for Kindness

We are beginning again. When we get to the end of
the story we shall know more than we do now.
                                    —*Hans Christian Andersen*

Some folks you respect, others you love.
        —*Karla Spurlock Evans, Dean of Multicultural Affairs,
                            Trinity College, Hartford, Connecticut*

April 1943

For the first time in years, I was happy. I loved having five
children to care for. They liked/loved me, each in their own way.
Yes, I still worried about my family. I had had no news. But I
remembered what my father said when he came home from
prison: "You are allowed to be happy, even if you're sad."

April 5, 1943, was like any other day at the Balls Park Residential Nursery. I had spent time singing and walking with my children and was ladling out tapioca pudding for lunch when Miss
Tilton asked me to come to her office. She set off alarm bells. Was
she going to let me go? And where would I go? But she smiled
and asked me to sit down, and after taking a deep breath said, "I
have a letter from Mr. Rattenbury who received a letter from your
uncle in Geneva." It was my turn to take deep breaths. "Your
father wrote that he and the family were being sent East." All I
could think of was, why had he been so confident about getting
a visa from our cousins in the United States? Why had he transferred our visa to a relative who was in need? Miss Tilton inter-
rupted my thoughts.

"Your father, from what you keep telling us, is brave. I am quite
sure that he will make contact with the partisans. No need to

worry. You are needed. The children are fond of you. Rest a minute and when you are ready, go back to the lunchroom."

When I returned, the children were still eating their pudding and the sun was still shining through the windows. Very few minutes had passed, but my world had changed. My family had disappeared. How could I go on?

The tears arrived while the children rested on their cots. "What's the matter?" asked Maureen. I was afraid to answer. The tears might become a torrent. By then, all of them were watching me, wondering. Billy knew. "Miss Eva has a tummy ache from eating too many sweets." That stopped the tears. To cheer me further, Maureen and Billy started singing one of their favorite versions of "Bah, bah black sheep, have you any bull, bull, bull?" The others joined in, singing "bull, bull, bull" as loud as their lungs would permit, obviously thinking the noisier the better. We had changed "wool" to "bull" during one of our singing sessions. Tears were still flowing, but I couldn't help laughing. They loved me. I loved them. My father's love for children was inside me.

Hours later I could not sleep. I needed a live human being. I put my coat over my nightie and drifted down four flights of stairs to the kitchen. The door was ajar, the light was still on, and I could see Mrs. Gerrety sitting in her rocking chair knitting. I watched her for a while, not knowing how to approach, and finally whispered, "Mrs. Gerrety." She was startled.

"Dear me," she said, "if it isn't Miss Eva. What are you doing up so late at night? Why, it's past midnight."

"I couldn't sleep."

"So glad you came. It gets a little lonely down here. I'll make us both some hot milk. It's too late for tea."

We shared the hot milk and munched a buttered crumpet.

"The war does make everything so difficult," she said. "That's why I sit up late and knit. Gets me untangled, if you know what I mean."

The hot drink and crumpet calmed my inside while Mrs. Gerrety did the talking.

"You see, I sit up late because I keep thinking of Seamus, my one and only son. He's on a destroyer far out at sea. I haven't heard from him lately." I didn't know what to say.

"I tell you what, Miss Eva," said Mrs. Gerrety. "Come down any time at all. I am usually up. I do love company."

She found an apple in the basket next to the stove.

"Here take this apple, and when you have tucked yourself in, take bites and chew well. It calms your nerves and cleans your teeth."

Then she handed me a colorful "Modern Romances" paperback entitled *Dancing in the Moonlight* from a pile of books and magazines next to her rocker.

"I know you love to read," she said. "This book tells the story of a lovely young girl a lot like you. Well maybe a year or two older, and the handsome sailor that she meets in Liverpool, and how they gradually fall in love. Have you ever been to Liverpool?"

Before climbing the stairs to my bedroom, I stepped outside into the night and took deep breaths while gazing at the stars and the crescent moon.

"Every living person needs a Tante Hans or a Mrs. Gerrety," I proclaimed out loud to the heavens.

Thursday, September 2, 1943, was my father's birthday. Birthdays were important occasions. I told Mrs. Gerrety that my father was fifty-three years old that day and asked her if she thought I would ever see him and the others again.

"Do you ever pray?" she asked me.

"Yes, I talk to der liebe Gott all the time."

"That's good, very good. Prayer is talking," smiled Mrs. Gerrety.

"I also say the *Shmah*, the prayer that means there is One God."

"You call Him 'der liebe Gott' don't you?"

It was my turn to smile.

"Well," she paused, "I will pray for you and your family, that you may all be reunited in time for your father's birthday next year."

I hugged her and thanked our One God for guiding me down those stairs and finding this kind, loving person.

After a year I realized that I had to move on. Loving children led me to believe I could help make sick children well and become a professional nurse, a step up from a helper. I hated saying good-bye to the children and Mrs. Gerrety. The lump in my throat almost choked me. "You come back," yelled Billie. Kevin nodded. Maureen was teary eyed. Mrs. Gerrety said, "Write." And I promised that I would.

Deportation to the East

By the time Eva learned that her parents and brother had been "sent East" most people knew that this did not mean conditions were going to be better. Many knew that the concentration camps existed, although they did not have any idea how horrible the conditions there were, nor that their main purpose was to enslave and kill people. The decision to kill all the Jews of Europe had been made by Hitler some time before January 1942, when the Nazi leaders held a conference at a resort known as Wannsee. There they created the details of their plan to round up, transport, and murder all the Jews under their control. They were already familiar with the processes for killing mass numbers of people.

The practice of killing those who were considered "unworthy of life" began in 1934. At first this meant sterilizing non-Jews who were "handicapped," such as those who were deaf or who had trouble walking due to childhood illnesses, like measles or polio. These innocent people were said to "pollute" the German "race," called the "Aryans." Later, the list included the mentally retarded and the mentally ill, and even juvenile delinquents.

When a massive protest from the Catholic Church forced the German government to stop this practice, it was continued in secret. By 1940, the methods used to kill handicapped and ill people were transferred to the death camps for the killing of Jews.

To keep the Jews from panicking and trying to go into hiding once orders had been posted announcing deportations, the government offered bribes of bread and marmalade, lied about jobs in the East, and sometimes resorted to threats of death (Schulz and Soumerai, 1998, 152). The procedure used for German Jews was usually quite civilized. They received written notification of "resettlement," and were told to lock up their valuables, carefully label the keys, and leave them on a table in their home. The penalty for refusing to do this was death. If families remained hidden in their homes they were hunted down, door by door, from one neighborhood to the next, dragged out, and beaten, sometimes killed immediately.

Paddington Green Children's Hospital

Love is a crude affair, there's 'drat the kid' in there, fatigue and lots of generosity. Neither late or early development means he's going to be a cabinet minister...

—*W. W. Winnicott*

A great man is he who has heart of a child.
—*Meng-Tzu, 372–289 B.C.*

At one glance
I love you
With a thousand hearts.

—*Mihri Hatun, (D. 1506)*

September 1943

On a Sunday in early September, I arrived at Liverpool Street Station in London and took a bus to the hospital located just off Edgeware Road. I scrambled to the top of the bus and enjoyed the view of London below: Oxford Street, Marble Arch, and finally "The Green" opposite the hospital where elderly ladies on benches watched children play hopscotch. Opposite was Paddington Green Children's Hospital, my destination. Above the entrance, a massive wooden door, a sculpture of a nurse cradling a baby fascinated me. That could definitely be me.

Matron Lilian Brooks welcomed me and wasted little time taking me upstairs to my room—a room all to myself with a view of the Green. She helped me carry my well-worn, treasure chest suitcase. "My goodness, this is heavy," she said. "You must have been places and seen things, I can tell." If she only knew, I thought. Staff Nurse Irene, soon to become my best friend, guide, and savior, knocked at my door a few minutes later and introduced herself. She was carrying a tray of sandwiches, a piece of pie, and a bottle of milk, and she led me to the nurses' sitting room where she switched on the electric heater, there being "a chill in the air," and suggested I make myself comfortable. It was her night off. "Relax, in the morning you will be ever so busy," were her parting words.

I sank into a well-worn armchair opposite the humming heater and turned on the radio next to the chair. I was very happy: music, food, children to love—who could ask for anything more? My parents and Norbert, we would all meet again after the war. And on that first night, I really believed we would.

I was too excited to sleep. The shade was up, the trees and stars visible. Tucked securely in bed and hugging my hot water bottle, I took inventory.

What did I need to lead the good life?

1. A window with a view—to connect me to God and my parents via stars and trees.
2. My own radio, right next to my bed—to listen to music and stories in the dark, to soothe me, to remind me of Papa tucking me in.
3. A library card—to connect me to goodness and help me understand evil.
4. A small bedside lamp in case the room is ugly—the lamp adds magic, like being in a Rembrandt painting.

Everything else was chance and could not be relied upon: good government, a nationality, a husband and children, a job you like, and pretty clothes. I decided to look into the library card the very next day. My personal radio and bedside lamp would take more than two years to get.

I loved wearing my nurse's uniform. I belonged. When on one particular night, fancy missiles known as "Doodlebugs" fell over Paddington and the injured were brought into the hospital, I, along with the nurses and doctors, worked around the clock to save, mend, repair, and comfort. We were valuable and valued members of a team, and I felt proud.

Reaching Out

There was something so special about the British. The London Underground stations, including Edgeware Road, were doubling as shelters. When returning late at night I would see folks huddling together, holding their babies and children in tight embraces. They were family. I belonged. Sometimes I would stay and sing with them made-up words. "We're too daft to know we have lost the war. Yes, together we will prevail."

The rush-rush aspect of my job did not bother me. I made do with the time I had, joked with the children, and told them stories while I attended to their needs. It was a case of juggling bedpans, hot water bottles, and compresses, serving food, making up beds, reciting nursery rhymes, and singing familiar songs, along with Mabel, our ward helper, who loved to hum an ancient song her mother had taught her about sunshine warming the "cockles of the soul." Singing made everyone happy, even those who were too sick to participate. They smiled along. So, apparently, did Dr. W. Winnicott, the world renowned children's psychiatrist, an attending physician at the hospital. During one of his visits he sought me out. "Nurse Eva, I always know when you are on duty."

"You do?" I couldn't believe my ears.

"I hear the children singing and I know. I hear them all the way downstairs." He laughed and so did his eyes. He had bushy eyebrows just like my father, and the crow's-feet around his eyes radiated with kindness. Then he asked me whether I would like to assist him in his clinic on Tuesday and Thursday afternoons. I wrote Uncle Karl in Geneva in great detail. Maybe he could find a way to transmit this good news to my parents.

I met Sammy, a fellow refugee from Vienna, at a dance for refugees and fell head over heels in love. After all, I was seventeen years old and entitled. The best walk/talk/concert of my entire life took place on a bright, breezy afternoon in midsummer 1943. Sammy and I met at the Marble Arch in the early afternoon, planning to amble along to Albert Hall to attend a promenade concert. Arm in arm, we strolled along the Serpentine, winding our way through Hyde Park and on to Kensington Gardens. We watched children float model boats on Round Pond and fly kites high up into the sky. We talked about religion.

Sammy was an orthodox Jew, I was liberal with personal connections to der liebe Gott, the creator of my good family and crocuses emerging through ice and snow. Sammy, who had watched his aging rabbi grandfather being forced to clean the sidewalk with his toothbrush, believed in ritual and frequent prayer. His favorite was called the *Amidah* because it included asking God for wisdom, the end of tyranny, and healing. We agreed that each of us is responsible for aiding in the healing process. "There are many more 'healers' than you think," added Sammy, embracing and kissing me with such dedication that it provided me with a giant push to become a healer full-time. We were crossing the Serpentine, and there, just past the bridge, was Peter Pan surrounded by his fairy tale friends, about to step off his pedestal "to Neverland." "He's been waiting a long time," said Sammy. We walked on and then suddenly, in the distance, we saw Prince Albert sitting in his Memorial opposite Albert Hall, our destination.

In a sudden burst of energy, I started running up the steps of the memorial, yelling to Sammy, "Beat me up there!" At the top of the steps he caught me and arm in arm we greeted the fellow German and beloved husband of Queen Victoria, who sat high above us in isolated splendor, staring at his catalog detailing the exhibition he had arranged. "The world is his. Too bad he died so young," said Sammy. Then we noticed across the street the thousands of people who seemed to be entering Albert Hall from all directions. We waved good-bye to Prince Albert, ran across the street, and entered the door to the pit.

We could only afford standing room but we were young and it was a pleasure. Music, I mused, was like life should be. The orchestra gave expression to the happy allegro movements as well as the sad/slow "largo/adante" ones. They all had a place and belonged, even though each one had its own theme, sometimes delicately stated by a lonely flute, sometimes a singing violin, and occasionally a powerful trumpet. Under the conductor's baton, dissonances dissolved and glorious harmonies evolved in a re-

"Riding out and away" from Paddington Green Children's Hospital.

statement of the themes in splendid affirmation. The audience cheered, loathe to leave at the end.

It must have been the warm summer night that made me add love words to the theme of Schubert's *Unfinished Symphony*, still ringing in our ears. "Sammy, I love you so, I love you so my darling Sammy . . ." And would you believe, at that very moment a shooting star dived through the sky toward us? And what's more, Bibi's Big Dipper (the pan without a lid) was clearly visible. "Let's make a wish," cried Sammy. I made two: one, to be eternally linked to Sammy, and two, to have my parents and Bibi attend our wedding. Who is to say that these wishes won't come true in another life?

I also loved eight-year-old Vi (Violet), a terminally ill child from London's East End who was dying of T.B. Meningitis. During the six weeks of life left to her, I spent every available minute, including all of my free time, at her side. I placed Angelika, my doll, right next to her so she did not have to turn. "Nursie" (that's what she called me), "Take me with you." I drew her picture in front of me and Bibi in the photograph of us riding the horse on our last vacation at Swienemuende and stuck it on a picture of the door of the hospital. We were leaving together, I promised her. And we did. When she died, I left nursing.

The War Comes to an End

In war: resolution. In defeat: defiance. In victory: mag-
nanimity. In peace: goodwill.

—*Winston Churchill*

1945

The war was almost won. I thought I could help in the healing
process by assisting chemists in the development of antibiotics
and penicillin, so I got a position at Glaxo Laboratories near London. I filtered penicillin through endless samples of charcoal and
kept careful notes. I also got lonelier by the hour; so lonely, in
fact, that I insisted on giving my doll Angelika to the chief chemist
when I heard he had six children. Maybe he would have me over?
I was in desperate need of children and laughter. It did not happen and I was too embarrassed to ask him to return Angelika.

At 2:41 AM on May 7, 1945, Field Marshall Gustav Jodl signed
Germany's unconditional surrender in Rheims, France. At the
same time the Supreme Commander of the Allied Forces, Dwight
David Eisenhower, born and bred in the small town of Abilene,
Kansas, made this victory announcement to the world: "The mis-
sion of this Allied force was fulfilled at 02:41, local time, May 7,
1945." This triggered incredible joy. Sammy and I celebrated at
Trafalgar Square. Surrounded by wildly cheering crowds, blowing
paper trumpets, and singing "Knees Up, Mother Brown," we
joined in dancing the Conga until the wee hours of the morning,
while Admiral Nelson, way up high on his pedestal, the lions,
and the pigeons displayed no surprise whatsoever. We sang and
were convinced that "there'd always be an England." England had
saved 10,000 children from certain death, something to be grateful
for—always.

Part IV

Searching for Answers

Displaced Persons

After the war there was no place to house the survivors of the concentration camps. Their homes had been stolen, their families were gone, and their neighbors, for the most part, did not want to see the Jews return. They were forced to stay in the camps, now being run by the Allies and the United Nations Relief and Rehabilitation Administration (UNRRA). Although much kinder than the Nazis, the Americans had hardly more resources to offer the inmates and conditions were deplorable. There was not enough medicine, housing, or clothing. And no one to help the survivors find their loved ones or try to return home. They were too quiet, they looked awful, they were visibly fearful, and their presence made others feel guilty. Many were sick or dying. A poll taken at the time showed that an overwhelming majority of the displaced persons, if not allowed to go to Palestine, "preferred gas chambers to going home." (293)

When General Eisenhower visited the camps, he demanded improvements, and President Harry Truman agreed. General George Patton, as supervisor of the camps, was not interested in doing anything to improve the suffering of the survivors, so Eisenhower had him removed. By Fall 1945, Jewish groups had been let into the camps and were setting up schools, providing aid, and training people to go to Palestine to create a Jewish state. Many survivors began to marry and start new families.

Allied Civilian Employee

Eyes are the mirrors of the soul.

—Anonymous

If life does not have meaning, make your life have meaning.

—Albert Camus

On October 10, 1945, I officially became an Allied Civilian Employee in the United States Army of Occupation and was assigned to the Civil Censorship Division Headquarters in Munich, Germany. A boat and a train, the reverse of what had brought me to England five years earlier, took me back to the now vanquished country of my birth.

We had an hour's stopover at Karlsruhe, the first German city on our itinerary, and I bounded out of the train to find somebody to talk to, to begin to find out what happened. I found an elderly man sipping a cup of ersatz coffee in the station restaurant. Feeling safe in my ACE American uniform, I asked whether I might sit with him. "*Natuerlich,*" (certainly) was his response. Little did I realize that this was the beginning of my life-long pursuit of the whys and wherefores of an event about to be called the Holocaust.

I introduced myself and told him my name was Eva. He was "Konrad" and he wondered whether I could spare a cigarette. I offered him one from my ever-ready-to-bribe-cajole package of Players. Konrad helped himself to two and told me that I spoke excellent German. "That's why I was chosen to go to Munich," I responded. Deeply inhaling the smoke, he informed me of the horrors Germany had suffered during the war. "Junge Dame" (young lady), "nobody suffered more. My youngest son Josef, an artillery officer in General Paul's Sixth Army, died in January '43

Reading and searching for "answers" and "goodness."

at Stalingrad. He died in ice and snow, in twenty-four degrees below zero temperature. He died a hero." He showed me a photo of a smiling German soldier with a swastika on his cap.

"What a tragedy. Did it have to happen?" I was looking for some sort of resulting wisdom and/or admission of responsibility. What Konrad said, however, was "It was not our fault. It was Adolf Hitler's fault. He wasn't even German. He was Austrian."

"And you could do nothing?" I asked.

"Nothing," he said. And suddenly I thought of Hubi, the glazier whose neighbors said and did nothing except bury Mimi and explain that he was a Communist. "A lot of people suffered," I said.

Konrad asked for another cigarette, and said, "How would you know, you were not living in Germany." The divide between us was too great to even begin a conversation, so I said, "My parents were living in Germany. They disappeared. We are Jewish." Konrad was speechless and forgot about his cigarette, which dangled unlit from his lips. I said good-bye.

In the train, I scribbled the conversation in my notebook and added the thought that these ready-made explanations from folks who were only concerned about their own well being and suffer-

Allied civilian employee ID photo, U.S. Army 1945/46.

ing would never make even a dent in ending suffering or injustice for those of us destined to inhabit this one world.

While my brief stopover in Karlsruhe gave me food for thought, reading about the liberation of the concentration camps in an old copy of *Life* magazine made me choke. Allied soldiers, liberating Dachau, spoke of the "unbearable stench, typhus, crawling skeletons, ditches of excrement and sunken eyes, home to maggots." It was an immediate and total immersion into the horrors of the camps. The maggots and the occasional smiles on a few faces have become fixtures in my mind's eyes. I wrapped myself in my coat and stared out of the train window. Stars were out in force and so was a golden harvest moon. How could the heavens be so beautiful and the world so ugly? But weren't the heavens part of the world? And where was der liebe Gott? Papa had assured me He was everywhere. And where were my parents?

I always seemed to operate in several worlds. In the Censorship Division world of Munich, I was soon promoted to "Allocation," where the important nuggets of information gathered by the censors were passed to us for proper "allocation" to appropriate agencies for action. These nuggets included hiding places of SS officers who had committed crimes against humanity and locations of stolen art treasures from "enemies" of the Reich or museums such as the Louvre.

I doubled my salary in three months, fell in love with peanut butter, and decided that, come what may, America was my des-

INFORMATION & RECORDS DEPARTMENT
GROUP "A", CIVIL CENSORSHIP DIVISION
UNITED STATES FORCES, EUROPEAN THEATER
APO 205   U S ARMY

23 August 1946

TO WHOM IT MAY CONCERN

    1. Miss Eva Nussbaum has been working in this Department from 11 October 1945.

    2. During this time she carried out her duties in an excellent manner, and contributed greatly in the forming of a new Department.

    3. Her sincere and straight forward manners won her a great number of friends, and she was liked and respected by everyone.

    4. Her immediate superiors judged her always as highly honest and trustworthy.

EMMERICH A EBER - WDE
Chief, IRD

Letter of reference from the U.S. Army, 1946.

tination. I acquired all the books I desired from the PX (army supply base), a bedside lamp, a bookshelf above my bed, and a radio.

Accompanied by new friends, I rode a white stallion (like Napoleon) at 5 AM, three times a week, and enjoyed a sumptuous breakfast each morning before going to work. That was the happy side that I was obliged to live to give me energy and to make a difference. That is what my father had said and had always demonstrated. I registered my family's names with the Red Cross and the United Nations' Relief Organization in the hope of locating them as soon as ever possible. In the meantime I found a kind American officer, Captain Allucino, who was willing to load his jeep with leftover supplies and drive with me to the Foehrenwald Displaced Persons' Camp.

Taking supplies to Foehrenwald Displaced Persons' Camp.

The first time we went was heartwrenching; to see skeletons on the loose, unloading our supplies, laughing. I didn't want them to laugh. Don't ask me why, except what had obviously happened to them was so terrible, that weeping was more in order than laughing. I was embarrassed. What was Joe (Captain Allucino) going to think. He did not comment but insisted on staying in his jeep, while I shared spaghetti with a survivor who explained the gas ovens and smells to me. I was unable to eat but gladly gave my portion to my new friend who was still hungry. His eyes, without maggots, were sunk in his skull, as though they did not wish to bear witness. I no longer wanted to find my parents or brother and felt overwhelming guilt.

I told Joe, who asked me why I was crying. He took my hand and said words I will remember to my dying day: "You mean to tell me that if you knew a member of your family was in this or that hospital, you would not go?" I said, "I would fly there, none could stop me," and thanked him.

We drove in silence. When we passed a playground, I asked him to stop. I hugged a child, a little German boy who had fallen off a swing. "Take your time," said Joe. A month later Joe went home to Brooklyn to marry his high school sweetheart. I wondered whether she realized how lucky she was. Before leaving, he told me how meeting me and the trips to Foehrenwald had made him realize what he had been fighting for.

In turn, Joe made me realize how dependent we are on one

Hugging a child on the way home from Foehrenwald.

another. How impossible it is to make it on your own. How kindness and understanding are the most important gifts we can bestow on one another. Joe represented "America the Beautiful" to me, the country I would one day call my own.

Jakov, survivor of Auschwitz, introduced himself to me by tapping me on the shoulder on my way to work one day. "It's nice to see a Jewish face," he said. "A Jewish face?" He just knew, he said. I liked him. I liked his energy, his forthrightness. He was short, maybe a little more than five feet. It helped him survive, he said; he could live on next to nothing. What also helped him was singing Yiddish *chochmes*, words of wisdom. I especially liked the ones he sang about the "soul." *"Di neshome ken men nit oys'shpayen"* (the soul can't be spat out) and *"Vi zeyf farn guf iz a trer far neshome"* (like soap for the body are tears for the soul).

We met a few times at the Hofbrauhaus, Hitler's hangout. We had survived, Hitler had not. It was up to us to do our share of *tikkun olam*, healing the world. Yakov defined evil for me. His father had begged the SS doctor in charge of selecting who lives and who dies to let them stay together. The butt of a gun smashed his father's glasses. Yakov's last view of his father was of him picking bits of glass out of his bleeding eyes on the way to the gas chamber. The other example was of a young, nursing mother sucking on an icicle as she entered a cattle car. A young SS man pushed it out of her mouth. "Why?" she asked. "Here, there is no why," was his response. "Who was she?" I asked. "She was my sister," said Yakov.

Yakov was leaving for Palestine. On the last day we met, he handed me a series of charcoal drawings drawn by a young prisoner. One entitled "If Only" shows a forlorn figure looking across a barbed wire fence into a distant sunrise. "If Only!" I vowed to do my very best.

Return

May the day come soon, the day for which we long,
when all humanity will recognize that it is one family.
—*Gates of Prayer, Central Conference
of American Rabbis*

Spring 1970

It took me thirty years to come home to Berlin. On the way, I stopped off in London to see Dr. Winnicott, who, in spite of having suffered several heart attacks, "looked forward to seeing me." He, alone, had understood why I had to leave the hospital after Vi's death and had assured me that children would always be part of my future. He was the one person I longed to see.

It had been more than ten years since I'd last seen him and I was shocked at how frail he looked. He ushered me into his study and suggested we enjoy a glass of sherry and watch the flames dart in and out of the crackling wood in the fireplace. Everything in his home spelled kindness—the sherry, the open hearth, the many books, a miniature farm complete with cows and chickens. "We have to get back to the simple things in life," he said and asked me what had happened to my family.

I told him my mother died in the concentration camp of Stutthof on January 5, 1945, my brother on May 13, a few days after the war ended. He and his buddy had been on a death march into Germany and were enjoying a swim in a lake when some returning soldiers noticed the tattooed numbers on their arms and shot both to death. Someone recorded the numbers and sent them to the authorities who turned them over to the Red Cross.

"People are better at noting and recording than at assisting," said Dr. Winnicott. He asked about my father. I told him I did not know what had happened to him and I did not want to find

COMITÉ INTERNATIONAL DE LA CROIX-ROUGE

SERVICE INTERNATIONAL DE RECHERCHES
3548 Arolsen · République fédérale d'Allemagne

INTERNATIONAL TRACING SERVICE	INTERNATIONALER SUCHDIENST
3548 Arolsen · Federal Republic of Germany	3548 Arolsen · Bundesrepublik Deutschland

Schm.

Téléphone: Arolsen 434 · Télégrammes: ITS Arolsen

Arolsen, den 12.März 1968

An die
United Restitution Organization

1 BERLIN-WILMERSDORF
Helmstedterstr.5

Unser Zeichen	Ihr Zeichen	Ihr Schreiben vom
T/D - 504 679	U 5517 u. U 5518	9. Februar 1956

Betrifft: NUSSBAUM geborene FABISCH, Frieda, geboren am 16.November
1899 in Berlin.

Sehr geehrte Herren!

Der nachstehende Bericht ist eine offizielle Ergänzung unserer Inhaf-
tierungsbescheinigung No.62053 vom 8.Juni 1956, die wir Ihnen am 13.
Juni 1956 übersandten:

> NUSSBAUM geborene FABISCH, Friedel, geboren am
> 16. November 1899 in Berlin, Staatsangehörigkeit:
> deutsch, Beruf: Arbeiterin, letzter Wohnort:
> Berlin, Lessingstr.10,
> wurde am 1.Oktober 1944 von der Sipo Riga in das
> KL-Stutthof eingeliefert, Häftlings-Nr.95328.
> Dort ist sie am 5.Januar 1945 um 13,00 Uhr verstorben.
> Todesursache: Herzmuskelschwäche.
> Kategorie oder Grund für die Inhaftierung:"Jüdin"
>
> Allgemeine Bemerkungen: Friedel = Frieda
>
> Geprüfte Unterlagen: Häftlingspersonalkarte und
> Todesmeldungen (3 x) des KL-Stutthof.

Sterbeurkunde ist beigefügt.

Hochachtungsvoll

U. Kocher

My mother's death certificate, stating cause as "heart muscle
weakness"; note the reason for internment is "Jewish."

out. I could not live with any more pain. My grandparents and
Tante Hans were deported to Terezin but never arrived.

From the small pile of books in front of him, Dr. Winnicott
picked up a copy of his best-selling book, *The Child and the Outside*

World, in German translation and wrote the following words inside: "An Eva, Kind, Donald W. Winnicott von der Umwelt 1970." He then wrote something different to me in several other books from the stack.

"I know you love books," he said. "Take them, and read them in good health." I could hardly speak. A few tears were cleansing my soul. "I will treasure them, always," I said, wondering whether he realized the difference he had made in my life. "God bless you," tumbled out of my mouth, making Dr. Winnicott laugh. "You used to be an agnostic, if I remember correctly." It was my turn to smile, "You are the one who told me I was not a case of arrested development."

Framed by the doorway, he said good-bye and words I will treasure always: "Keep being yourself, sometimes angry and, let's be honest, occasionally untidy, but always loving. It's a wonderful mix, you know. Those in your care will thrive."

A few hours later I asked a taxi driver in line at the Berlin airport to take me to Lessingstrasse 10, as though I had never left. "What brings you here?" And I told him. I wanted the whole world to know: "You see, I am Jewish and was sent to England on the Kindertransport. I lost my entire family. My grandmother was blind. Nobody survived. Why? you might ask. That's what I ask myself every day. I used to live at Lessingstrasse 10."

The taxi driver stopped the meter and told me his name was Heinrich. "I'll stay with you," he said. "I know the neighborhood. I grew up there." It turned out we both went to the Bochumerstrasse elementary school.

Coincidence or miracle, I wasn't sure which, but the only prewar house still standing on that street was number 10. It looked exactly as I remembered it, only much smaller.

I leaned against the taxi and stared at the window—the Crystal Night window. I told Heinrich that's where we stood the night they burned the synagogues. And there, where it says "Drugs," was the laundry and Frau Mueller. "Take all the time you need, I'll wait for you," said Heinrich.

I walked through the same wooden door and up the stairs. And there, on the first floor on the left, was our apartment. There was

Our apartment house and the Crystal Night window.

a sign on the door. It said: "COME IN." It was a doctor's office. Our front hall was now a reception room. A nurse sat at the desk where the mahogany mirror and the umbrella stand had once stood. I explained that this had been our home and would she mind if I looked around. She did not. Office hours were in the afternoon. I had a whole hour before patients were scheduled.

My parents' bedroom was the waiting room. How apt. There once had been angels floating on the ceiling. How often had I looked at them while Papa told Bibi and me stories on a lazy Sunday morning, as Mama stitched away on that old creaky Singer sewing machine and Tante Hans ground coffee beans, sending waves of delicious aroma into the air. The doctor's private office was my former bedroom, which had been our dining room until we had to sell all the furniture.

The Crystal Night window was slightly open. I looked through the crack and noticed Heinrich, leaning against his taxi, looking up. I don't know why, but I waved and he waved back. How ironic life was. There he was, my new friend, eager to help me in any way he could. And once upon a time, while I was crying my eyes out in England, he must have been a proud member of the Nazi youth movement.

On the other side of the hall was our living room, now the examination room. The same sun was sending its last rays through the window as it had all those years earlier, when my family had gathered at the table sharing "good" news and watching Papa's Camembert cheese "run." I missed the chestnut tree and found out that it had been cut down.

The pain, the loneliness, the sorrow of all those in-between years lent an unexpected depth to the love and gratitude I felt for those good people—my family—who had loved me and each other. They must have sat in front of this window to write to me almost every day. It occurred to me that throughout my life I had searched for evidence of goodness, and here it was, in this spot. My mother would send me bits of poems mixed in with advice while my brother told me how much he missed me and sent me anywhere from one to one hundred kisses. He had been the only wage earner those last few months. I felt such pride for him. My loyal, loving father became the source of comfort, as always. I felt he was there beside me, putting his arm around me and helping me grieve for my mother and brother—and all those millions of mothers, fathers, brothers, and sisters.

Heinrich asked me how I could come back, knowing what had happened. You don't understand, I told him, visiting my childhood home was like a blessing. That's where I once belonged and was loved, where we sat and argued, where, during Crystal Night, my father helped a stranger, and where he told so many stories that I became a lifelong listener. If I could tell a burly Berlin taxi driver my innermost feelings, I could do anything, I thought. After a while he said, "I could have been you and you could have been me. It all depended how we were born. We even went to the same school." I told him about the cape I wore at school to hide my trembling arms during the Nazi salute. He was surprised. Had I been that frightened?

Heinrich showed me three stumps on his left hand. "Frostbite, Stalingrad," he said. Then he added that Russians are people, too,

A poem Uncle Adolf sent me from Belgium: . . . are a real wonder child / will do honor to England / beautiful greetings from / Onkel Adolf, Tante Hete and a / 1,000 wows-wows from Buffi / now rest your head. . . .

"they bleed when they are shot and freeze in subzero temperature." He had not known any Jews. There were none in his class. He had never thought about Jews. There was so much going on in his life. Youth group meetings, and, yes, there were hate songs during the many marches on weekends, but to be honest, he thought mostly about marching to the beat. "By the time there is a war, everybody rallies round the flag. Most of us trusted our leadership. Who were we to question? We were like a bunch of flag-carrying sheep who love order, spiffy uniforms, and marching in step."

He gave me his address and said, should I return, he would be pleased to have me stay with his family and children. "It's education we need," he said.

"I wish it were that simple. Many Ph.D.s, physicians, trained

Aunt Hete and I celebrate our "good" family.

engineers, even philosophers, helped in the extermination efforts. They also loved their families, roses, and walks in the park."

"If it's not education, what is it?"

"It is also education, but maybe meeting each other, one on one, helps."

"Perhaps at the airport."

"And switching off the meter."

"That's it," laughed Heinrich.

I had one more treat, meeting my Tante Hete, who had emigrated to Brussels to start a new life with my mother's brother Onkel Adolf and their terrier Buffi, whom Adelheid and I had loved to walk. All went well for them until the Germans invaded Belgium and offered the local population a few francs or five pounds of sugar for giving a Jew's name to the Gestapo. There were plenty of takers, similar to the case of Anne Frank in Holland. Hete waited for her husband in Brussels for two years after the war, just in case he would return.

Aunt Hete, her husband Adolf, and their terrier Buffi shortly after their wedding, 1938.

We drank a toast to each other and the happy times we had shared with my family and her "ever young" husband, who had sent me a Buffi poem when I was so lonely in England. I was reminded of an ancient prayer thanking "Der liebe Gott," something my parents would have liked.

> We are thankful for the companionship that continues
> in a love stronger than death. . . .
> —*Gates of Prayer*

Postscript

My mother gave me a love for books, the heavens, and earth. She said I was willful. She was right. I always wanted to know more than was required and invented programs that were not part of the syllabus. My father introduced joy into my life at a very early age. I learned that laughter is the shortest distance between two people and helps sell initiatives. My brother demonstrated that immaturity has nothing to do with character. He put food on the table until they were all deported in the winter of 1943.

To the above mix, add the experiences of an all-encompassing loneliness, a confrontation with evil, a love for children, and a belief in the existence of goodness, and you get a strong desire to communicate all these feelings to others to "heal the world."

For forty years I have worked with children, in at least as many settings. I have taught them to be proud, to help and respect one another, and to have fun. I have done this through the vehicle of multimedia tributes to inspirational individuals, such as Anne Frank, Langston Hughes, and Dona Felisa Rincon, the first woman mayor of San Juan, Puerto Rico. Besides helping students practice reading, writing, and thinking, creating these tributes suggests that we are all responsible for the choices we make, and that our choices affect others, coming back to strengthen us or to haunt us. Students and teachers assist in this process and become part of our "family." I am seventy-five years old and am still doing tributes. I have found that life is easier when you are surrounded by plain goodness, intelligence, and friendship.

Glossary

Allied Powers.   Countries that fought with the United States and England against the Axis Powers.

Axis.   Countries that joined with Germany to fight the Allies.

Concentration Camps.   Places where Jews and others who were considered "enemies of the state" by the Nazis were held as prisoners-of-war, forced to work as slaves, or murdered.

Final Solution.   Term used for the deliberate annihilation of the Jewish people.

Gestapo.   The extremely brutal Nazi Secret State Police who were not subject to review by any court.

Goebbels, Paul Joseph (1897–1945).   Nazi propaganda minister. Hitler's most loyal associate.

Goering, Hermann (1893–1946).   Second in command of the Third Reich. He gave the order to begin the Final Solution.

Himmler, Heinrich (1900–1945).   Leader of the SS, chief of the German Police, and absolute authority over the concentration camps.

Hitler, Adolf.   Founder and leader of the Nazi party, and Fuehrer of

Germany from 1933–45. Born in Austria on April 30, 1889. In his book, *Mein Kampf* (My Struggle), he laid out his racist and anti-Semitic theories and his plans to take over Europe, enslave the Poles, and kill all the Jews.

Holocaust. Greek word for "total burning." Holocaust refers to the murder of approximately 6 million Jews between 1933 and 1945, by the Nazis and those who aided them. Some people also use the term to refer to the systematic murder of thousands of Gypsies and other innocent civilians by the Nazis.

National Socialist German Workers' Party (Nazis). The political party that began as the German Workers' Party and was taken over by Hitler.

Schutzstaffel (SS, protection squads). Elite military arm of the Nazi party.

Sturmabteilung (SA, storm troopers, Brownshirts). Street fighters who helped Hitler come to power. In June 1934, Hitler had their leaders murdered because their rowdy actions embarrassed his government.

Third Reich. Hitler's "empire." He believed the first Reich was the Holy Roman Empire, the second, the Empire of Germany under Bismarck.

Questions for Discussion and Reflection

Universal Questions

Each chapter in this volume is headed by quotations from writers, philosophers, and statesmen and stateswomen. The passages talk of duty and dishonor, loyalty and betrayal, courage and cowardliness, power and its abuses. Most important, they speak of the need for family and friends to help us make meaning of our lives. Each quotation is directly related to the events in the chapter, and can serve as a jumping-off point for thoughtful discussion and writings about these ideas and issues.

Departure

1. Imagine you are forced to leave home during wartime, knowing you may never see your family again. Record your thoughts and feelings.

2. What do you think Eva's parents talked about when deciding to send her to England?

3. Research the United States' response to Hitler's treatment of the Jews in the 1930s. Our government voted against taking in Jewish children from Germany. Find out why it made this decision. Do you agree or disagree with its actions?

Part I: Back to the Beginning

4. Write about an early memory you have of doing something special with a parent or other close relative. Discuss why you think the memory has stayed with you.

5. Ask your parents or grandparents if they have any family stories from before you were born.

6. During the 1920s many Americans, and even some wealthy Europeans, began to buy cars. Do some research on other appliances or machines that were invented at that time or just becoming affordable. Which ones had the potential to save lives? Today there is also lifesaving technology that some can afford and others can't. Do you think the government should guarantee these things for everyone?

7. Write a journal entry about something you learned from a parent or close relative that you think you will remember when you are an adult.

8. Collect some favorite family recipes that you could include in a class cookbook. Perhaps this can be used as a fundraiser and the money could be used to help refugees.

9. If you know someone who has served in the armed forces during a war, see if he/she is willing to be interviewed about his or her experiences. Write your questions ahead of time so you are prepared. Ask the veteran how he/she would react if the U.S. government arrested innocent members of his/her family because of race or religion.

10. Research the Hitler Youth program in Germany in the 1930s. Who was in it? What were they taught? How were they expected to behave? Look up the life of Sophie Scholl and her brother. They were members of the Hitler Youth who later joined a resistance group to fight against the Nazis.

11. Have you ever been betrayed by a close friend? How did you feel? What happened? What was the cause of this betrayal? Did you ever become friends again? Did this make it hard for you to make other close friends again?

12. If someone rang the doorbell and asked you for help, what would you do?

Part II: Holding On

13. Imagine you are Eva and write a diary entry about your last day with your family.

14. Imagine you are separated from your family for an undetermined

period of time. What experiences from your past would you recall that could help you be less sad?

15. If you had to leave your home and family for a year, what would you take with you?

16. What are some of the rules you have in your house? Do you think the rules Eva had to obey were fair? Why do you think she disobeyed her foster parents?

17. Explain the irony in Eva's first meeting with the other girls at recess.

18. React to "Uncle's" reasons for making Eva return the tennis equipment.

19. If you could write a letter to Eva, now or when she was thirteen, what would you tell her? What would you ask her?

Part III: Reaching Out

20. How does Eva overcome her sadness? Why does she leave nursing? What does she learn during this period in her life?

Part IV: Searching for Answers

21. Whom does Eva blame for the war?

22. What does Eva learn from Joe? From Yakov?

23. What did Heinrich the taxi driver mean when he said: "By the time there is a war, everybody rallies around the flag. Most of us trusted our leadership. Who were we to question? We were like a bunch of flag-carrying sheep...." Do his words have any relevance to us today?

Making Choices: More to Think About

Nicholas Winton, one of the people who made the Kindertransport possible, said this about the efforts of those who were willing to reach out and save children, and those who chose not to participate:

> Maybe a lot more could have been done, but much more time would have been needed, much more help would have been needed from other countries, much more money would have been needed, much more organizations.
>
> We may say the same thing in a few years' time about what's happening now in Yugoslavia [or any other troubled area of the world]. "Nobody learns anything; that's the only thing that history teaches us." (Harris and Oppenheimer, 2000, 258)

Do you agree?

Sources Used

Harris, Mark Jonathon and Deborah Oppenheimer. *Into the Arms of Strangers: Stories of the Kindertransport*. New York: Bloomsbury Publishing, 2000.

Soumerai, Eve Nussbaum and Carol D. Schulz. *Daily Life during the Holocaust*. Westport, CT: Greenwood Press, 1998.

Souvenir Brochure: A Reunion of Kindertransport 50th Anniversary, 1939–1989. Kindertransport Association, 1989.

"Winton's Wartime Gesture." *Jerusalem Post* (August 31, 1998).

Index

About the Authors

EVE NUSSBAUM SOUMERAI is an author, lecturer, teacher, and Holocaust survivor. She is the author of many publications including *Human Rights: The Struggle for Freedom, Dignity and Equality* (1998) and *Daily Life During the Holocaust* (Greenwood, 1998), both of which she coauthored with Carol Schulz.

CAROL D. SCHULZ has been a teacher of history and English for 24 years. She currently serves as the Language Arts Coordinator for a regional school district in Connecticut.